Secrets, Lies
and
Life Lessons

by

Isabella Rothbury

Secrets, Lies and Life Lessons

Disclaimer: This is a work of non-fiction. I have tried to recreate events and conversations from my memories of them. To protect the privacy of certain individuals their names and have been changed.

Edited by Donna Celiano

Cover design by Wayne Rothbury

Printed in the United States of America

ISBN-13: 978-1975710033
ISBN-10: 1975710037

In Memory

Mom, I miss you.   (Oh yeah, and the peanut butter and jelly sandwiches you made daily for me.)

Dedication

I would like to dedicate this book to my husband, Wayne. He is without a doubt the most amazing person in my life. He has been my companion, friend and teacher on our journey throughout life together.   He has held me, encouraged me, taught me, guided me, supported me, laughed at me and yes, even scuffed at me at times. Thank you for teaching me to see everything through a microscope.

To my family, without whom I would not have been able to write this book. Thank you for all your support, love and input. Especially my four siblings, Gregory Jr, Susan, Brian and Diane. As children of divorce, we were all subject to separation, hardships and disappointments. May we one day be reunited and find the happiness we sought as children.

** WARNING **

This book is intended for mature audiences as it contains material that some people may find disturbing and offensive.

Table of Contents

Prologue

It was my husband, Wayne, who encouraged me to research my family tree. Having done it before, he knew it would involve hours of gathering photos, documents, records, newspaper clippings and more. By using my family's tree, secrets and lies as examples, it has not only helped me understand who I am, but why I am the person, I am today.

Acknowledgements

I would like to take this opportunity, personally thanking the following people for their help, knowledge and inspiration in the writing of this book.

First, a big thank you goes to my family and Wayne's family.

I am also particularly grateful to my cousin Annie who listened to, encouraged me and was the inspiration for this book.

In addition, a very special thank you goes to my husband, Wayne. He wears the title of soulmate, computer guru and support person. He also designed and then constructed the book cover. How did I ever get so lucky?

Acknowledgments must also go to Dreamstime LLC for providing the photo of the scared girl. Moreover, to Al Parrish of Popular Woodworking Magazine who provided the stairway accent table image found on the book cover.

Preamble

Ralph Waldo Emerson once said,

"The only person you are destined to become is the person you decide to be."

That quote led me to think long and hard about my life and myself. It was then with the encouragement of my cousin, Annie, that I gained the courage to put my memoirs on paper. She had been suggesting for years that I should write a book. Time and time again, Annie was a patient listener as we talked endlessly about my life. Then while I was on the phone with her one day, she said, "Think about it. It would be good therapy for you. You need to let go of the pain, begin the healing process and help others while you're at it."

"But", I thought, "Would people understand the person I once was, versus the person I had now become?"

When I first brought up the idea of writing a book about family secrets in which I used our family as an example, I thought for sure my family would disown me. Instead, I found love, encouragement and support.

I knew exposing my family's secrets, lies and personal demons, which had been long buried deep within, would come with a price. I also believed I had finally come to a point in my life where I was ready to pay that price. I was finally ready to be master of my own destiny and seize control. I had gone to such great lengths for years trying to hide that side of "me" for so long. Now, I would be openly providing every detail in the hopes that I would find closure and healing for others as well as myself.

Most families have skeletons in their closets. So why do we go to such extremes to hide and afterwards tell secrets and lies about them? There are many reasons. Some people feel they are protecting someone. For others the desire to hide those secrets and lies will bring about guilt and shame if the truth were to surface. Still more do it to avoid conflict with some facing the stigma of being labeled or the loss of a job. Likewise, many years ago we simply just did not talk about things like sexual assault, domestic violence, teen pregnancy, alcoholism, mental illness, suicide or sexual preference. So when I chose to reveal some of my own family's secrets and lies to help others as well as myself, it was not an easy decision by any means. My family and friends at first thought I was crazy for doing it. Maybe I am! However, my goal in writing this tome is to give others *the permission to unlock that door and confront their skeletons head on.* To take charge of your life, past, present, future, and move forward. Do not let the secrets and lies of the past weigh you down, but soar with the lessons learned from them and move forward. If you do not believe that secrets can kill, lies can destroy and labels can cripple .... **just keep reading**.

Chapter 1

In the beginning

Wayne & Isabella on their wedding day, June 09, 2001

Call it destiny, fate, karma or whatever you want, but in the end, it was meant to be. My closet was full of skeletons, secrets and lies. So naturally, when I first met my second husband, Wayne, I was afraid to tell him "my life's story". Wayne was a good, Christian man. I worried that I maybe giving him too much information at first. Would these things overwhelm him with fear and scare him off? I was sure he would pack his things and run as fast as he could in the opposite direction. However, to my surprise and amazement, he did not. Instead, he proposed to me. Clearly, one or maybe both of us were crazy. The question was which one? Little did I know though that my whole world was about to come crashing down, and that he, only he, would remain my Rock of Gibraltar.

I first met Wayne when I was beginning my career in law enforcement. I had just obtained a Bachelor's degree in criminal justice from Saginaw Valley State University and needed two things; a life insurance policy and a will. Strange things you might think at first, but for those entering this field they were a necessity. I began by looking through the telephone directory in search of an insurance agent. I started with the A's and the first one I called was busy. I tried the next one that was a well-known insurance company. After a few brief questions, I was transferred to an agent named Wayne Rothbury. Mr. Rothbury arranged to meet with me later that week at my apartment to go over different types of life insurance policies. Once there he went over several policies and found one that would that would work for me. He also informed me that he had a legal program that would create a will for me, which I could borrow. I was elated to find out that I could get both things done at the same time.

Mr. Rothbury, who I was by now calling Wayne, was an extremely friendly and outgoing person. On our very first visit, I felt comfortable and at ease with him. It was easy to become his friend. He held nothing back, nor did he try to hide anything. This was a far cry from the tangled mess I had just come from.

My divorce from Todd, my first husband, had been messy and while I was not interested in a relationship, I did need a good friend; Wayne proved to be just that. Throughout the twelve years that followed, we stayed in touch with one another to talk about my policy and just see how the other was doing. It was not until January of 2001, when I was about to have surgery that I contacted Wayne with a question about my policy and found out that he was moving to Maryland. I panicked for I thought I might be losing my agent, he quickly assured me that he could continue to be my agent, even if he were almost 500 miles away. He also mentioned that he was having a garage sale to get rid of some items before moving. I inquired if he happened to have a twin bed because I needed one for my guest room. His answer was, "Yes". I headed over the next day to see him. After a little while, I decided to venture and ask him again about his move to Maryland. I was curious to see if he was really sure about making such a big move. I knew he had been a master gardener for a long time and had a love for flowers and gardening, so now he would have the opportunity to move near his oldest daughter, Elizabeth, and work on the family farm.

Ellen, his first wife, to whom he had been married for 34 years, had died in February of 1996 of breast cancer. They were blest with five wonderful children, all of which had left home by now. This was truly not only an opportunity for him to do something he loved, but also be closer to some his family. While I was happy for his fresh new start, I worried about losing my agent and longtime friend. He again assured me he would be able to continue on as my agent, and would most likely be making trips back to Michigan. We ended up going out to dinner that night. I shared more details about my life with him than I probably should not have. What impressed me most was that he did not back off or scare away at my openness and honesty. Moreover, when I went to kiss him goodbye, he said, "When can I see you again?" That was the beginning of a long distance relationship that lasted nearly six months. Wayne would travel back and forth from Maryland to Michigan, nearly 1000 miles at a time, to be with me. As a result of that kiss, I decided that I would be totally open and honest with him.

One night while he was visiting me, we began talking about my life.

"Have you ever thought about researching your genealogy?" he asked.

"No, I haven't" I admitted. "

"You should do it. I think it would help you put things in perspective and give you some of the answers you are seeking. " he said.

I took his advice and soon I was at the computer day and night. Researching and digging to find the answers to the secrets and lies in my family and the lessons learned.

"Are you ever going to leave that computer?" he questioned another day.

All I could do was laugh and remind him that he was the one who started me down this path in the first place.

Chapter 2

Genealogy 101 (Black Sheep #1)

1st row R-L Hanna, Margaret
2nd row R-L Francis, Suzanne, Judy

I knew right from the very beginning there was going to be a dark side to researching my family. After all, that was to some extent what I was writing about, but it still did not prepare me for what I was about to find.

Our wedding day of June 9th 2001 was fast approaching and what time I was not spending on wedding preparation was on genealogy research. It was addictive! I had to know all there was to know about my ancestry.

Wayne was visiting me one weekend when he asked with a grin on his face, "How's the research coming? Any deep dark secrets I should know about before I marry you?"

"Well, since you asked, are you really sure you want to know everything? Because it is turning out to be complicated. *Very* complicated!" I said.

With a cup of coffee in hand (as usual) and still smiling he said, "So where do we begin?"

"Let me go get everything." I said, as I disappeared into the other room. When I returned, I could see that he had made himself comfortable on my sofa. I had retrieved a large "bag" full of legal records, documents, photographs and other items all of which had something to do with my life in one way or another. As I sat down next to him, and began to spread everything out in front of us, I could not help but laugh and think, "My life literally reminds me of a puzzle that has yet to be put together". It was then that I warned him that this was going to take a while. After all, there was just so much to go through that I did not know where to begin.

I decided to start with my mother; she was by far the most interesting and notorious in my family. Margaret, or "Maggie", as she was known, was born in Fenton, Michigan the fourth of five sisters. She and her four sisters, Judy, Francis, Hanna and Suzanne, would also grow up in that small town. It was the *things* Maggie did as a young woman that got everyone's attention. She became known as the "*Black Sheep*" of the family early on. At fourteen, she ran away to join the circus because she did not get her way at home. It was only by chance that her Father, Phillip, went there to look for her and found her hiding under one of the circus wagons. Had he not thought to look there, she would not have been seen again. Everyone makes choices in life and Maggie made some rather unusual, and controversial ones based solely on secrets and lies. What really made her decide to run away that day? No one knows. As you can image, her Father gave her a strong tongue lashing, grounded her for a couple of weeks and watched her closely from then on. Was this just a teenager testing her boundaries or was she on her way to becoming the "Black Sheep" of the family?

Maggie went on to make choices later in life that not only destroyed lives and careers, but also tore families apart.

These choices ended up affecting not only herself, but her children, her spouses, and many others around her. This domino effect caused numerous people to carry unnecessary guilt long after she was gone. One such "event" that I am aware of occurred before I was even born.

Maggie was about to graduate from high school, but she was more interested in her sister Francis's boyfriend, Gregory Dempsey As it so happened, Francis and Gregory broke up around this time and Francis started dating Howard Henderson who later became her husband. This left Gregory available to date Maggie. It wasn't long after that they began dating. In October of 1951, they would marry in Newark, New York before a US Air Force Chaplain. Gregory went on to join the U.S. Air Force where he trained as an aircraft mechanic. He then served in England during the Korean conflict. They would go on to have three children, Gregory, Susan and Brian. With, Brian, the youngest, being born in late 1959. Then in May of 1960, Maggie filed for a Divorce. Something that was at that time all but unheard of, because in those days families normally stayed together no matter what – for the benefit of 'the family'

The following was taken from Maggie's and Gregory's Bill of Complaint for Divorce that was filed with the Genesee County Court on May 09, 1960. (This would have been the 1st step of a divorce in those days where you would petition the court asking for a divorce and listing the reasons and requests) In those records, she claimed that:

> Her husband was guilty of extreme cruelty towards her. She further stated that he physically pushed and struck her, using foul, obscene, and vulgar language in front of her and the children.

> According to the records, Gregory was said to have disregarded the solemnity of the marriage vow obligations. Due to his actions, she claimed, there was so much constant and unbearable turmoil in the home that she became extremely nervous, lost weight, and had to consult with a doctor.

> Margaret went on to ask the court to end the marriage, give her temporary and eventually permanent custody of the children, a reasonable sum of alimony for support of herself and the children, a property settlement. [R1]

After the divorce there was not much personal property to divide; only an automobile, some household furniture, and personal effects. Since Gregory was steadily employed and Margaret had no income of her own, this now left Margaret without funds to prosecute the divorce, pay attorney fees, and miscellaneous expenses of litigation, as well support herself and the children. Considering that her husband was the "breadwinner" in the family, with a take home pay of $90 a week, he was asked to pay the fees and provide for her and the children.

Maggie is granted temporary custody of all three children until the divorce is granted on December 19, 1960. At that point, custody of the two older children is awarded to their father and the youngest is awarded to his mother. However, she keeps him for only a brief period of time, and then without Gregory's knowledge places him into the foster care. Approximately two years later, Gregory's father, Devin, learns where his grandson is and becomes furious with him for "abandoning his third child". He insisted that Gregory own up to his "family responsibilities". He threatened to "disown him and strike him from his last will and testament if he did not go out into the community, find and return his son to his own family." Fortunately, Gregory was successful in finding young Brian who was by that time in his second foster home.

Now here is where there are some discrepancies and it is where it gets even more convoluted.

By April of 1961, Gregory had fallen in love and married his second wife, Melissa. She would go on to raise the children as her own and provide them with a lifetime of love and stability. I cannot begin to say how much I admire and respect her for this.

On September 17, 1962 an Order was entered granting custody of the youngest child, Brian to the father. The parties agreed to the change in custody and the mother was given reasonable visitation.

Now, here, as Margaret begins to tell people that she had since remarried. A fact that was not true – and for which I will go into more detail later. The man she claimed as her husband was Neil Zimmerman .... my biological Father.

It was in February or March 1966 that my Father, Neil Zimmerman who was a police officer with the Flint Police Department, went to the Court Investigator's Office to inquire about Margaret's visitation rights with regards to the children. Court records indicate that she would be happy to have the two older children with her for one Sunday per month for the time being. (The investigator in charge thought this was odd since Margaret had not contacted him since the judgment was granted back in 1960.)

The following information was taken from *Amended*

Custody Records between Margaret and her first husband Gregory that were filed with the Genesee County Court on Aug. 28, 1966. Once you read it, you will understand its importance.

The children's father was contacted, and he reluctantly agreed with the suggestion of the court saying that the children should go to the home of their Mother on the first Sunday of one month, and the first Saturday of the alternate month. The father's reluctance in this matter was due to the fact that the children had not had contact with their mother in four or five years. He was also very concerned about their youngest child, Brian, as he had not been told that the stepmother was not his natural mother. Therefore the father did not want the mother having visiting rights relative to that child.

Both parties appeared in the investigator's office for the purpose of getting the visitation problem settled. At that time, the father told the mother that he was concerned about the welfare of the children and what the visits might do to their youngest child in particular. The parties could not agree and were advised to contact their attorneys. According to the mother, the two children enjoyed their visits with her and had expressed their wish to stay longer.

On August 24th, the investigator questioned the children. They denied they wanted to be with the mother more often or for a longer period of time. They said they were satisfied with things the way they were now. The oldest son stated that he thought his younger brother should not be included in the visitations and when asked why, he answered, "Why should he have to go through this?"

The children denied that either their father or their step-mother had said things against their mother. Since the parties could not agree on this matter, and were advised to contact their individual attorneys.

Margaret had stated that she had not tried to exercise her visitation rights due to the attitude toward the child's father and his present wife (Melissa). Instead the mother was now seeking custody of the youngest child and proposed the home in which she and my father, Neil Zimmerman were now living. The six roomed house was located on the East side of Flint and appeared to be acceptable. Other occupants of the home were myself, currently two years old at the time, child of the mother's present marriage, and my half-sister, Diane Zimmerman, age eighteen, and daughter of Father's previous marriage to Connie Gruner.

If Margaret were to receive custody of the youngest son, he would attend Freeman School.

It was the opinion of the Investigator and all others involved, that Margaret could not possibly have a sincere interest in the welfare of her youngest son when she was willing to separate him by asking for custody of just him and not the others.

It was also decided that all three children had been receiving excellent care in a good moral home, and to change custody would not be in their best interest.

It was recommended that the custody of the three minor children remain with their father. It was also recommended that the two older children spend one weekend per month with their mother, Margaret and Sunday on the second weekend of the month. It was also recommended that the children spend alternate holidays with the mother, and one week during the summer vacation; said week not to conflict with the children's camp activities. The visitation was to exclude the youngest son.

It was further recommended that neither the mother, Margaret nor her current husband Neil, enter the home of the first husband, or that he nor the present mother enter the home of the mother, Margaret.

It should also be noted here that according to the divorce document she was not guilty of the same misconduct or offenses that he was charged with as far as their marriage vows and obligations. [R2]

As stated before, it was now that she began living with my biological father, Neil Zimmerman, and it was then that she thought she might get her life together. She was so sure in fact, that she wrote the following letter to her father, Phillip and his second wife, Caroline. The letter was dated July 8, 1965.

Dear Dad and Caroline,

This is about the second letter I have written since I came home from England, so you two better feel lucky. And Dad I still can't spell worth a damn, but I sure will give it the good old English try! It seems since we have a house everything is going good for us, for the first time in my life, I can say it's so good to have a home and family. It's really something to enjoy every day and to find and have pride and self-satisfaction in my days' work and for once in myself. This I'm very proud about, and hope you feel the same about me after all these years. When your growing up it seems, I know when I was little, there were a lot of things I thought you were very hard on me, but believe me with all my heart. I thank you for trying to teach me right from wrong, but believe me I've never forgotten any of these things, but am know grown up enough to understand, and you will never know how hard I've tried in the last two years to better myself not first for me, but always in the back of my mind thinking someday my father can sit back and say I'm proud of her. And I hope and feel you can say it now. Because I'm very proud of you and always have been. (You no longer have a black sheep in your family!) By the way, Neil and I plan to (by law) be married within the next two months which will make me very happy. We picked up your clock last night, It works real good, I first had to try it and we're not sure yet but we're thinking about going up North the last week of this month, if we can. I will call you, for sure a week before so we can meet somewhere in between. Neil has next weekend off, so we might take a drive up there. But I'll let you know for sure when we're coming or (going) Ha-Ha. I hope Caroline you will enjoy your job. Sounds like fun.

Love, Maggie

P.S. By the way Caroline I think you're a mighty fine gal also, and hope you'll take care of that (bull headed Englishman-Ha Ha) for us, you should have him trained in the next 10 years! Ha Ha (R-G duns!) away from him! Ha-Ha that will do the trick! [R3]

This was clearly a side of my Mother that I had never seen before. My eyes teared up as I read the words. She was desperately seeking more than just approval from her Father. He had raised all his girls to be good, respectful, first class citizens. Yet, she at a very young age, was labeled the black sheep of the family. What went wrong and why was she unable to make it right? Both she and I would struggle for a lifetime with these questions.

I never thought of my mother as a "mother figure". You see, raising children was not on her list of priorities, yet, she had four of them. And as I look back on her life, I still wonder again, "What went wrong?" She started out with good parents and even had a good up-bringing. Lots of love, an education, all the "things" that you would think are necessary to turn out right, yet, she seemed to take the wrong paths. She ended up marring three times throughout her lifetime, and each one ended in divorce. Does that tell us something? I think so. Especially if we look at the men she married and the circumstances surrounding the divorces.

Her first marriage lasted only nine years before she ultimately filed for a divorce, blaming all the problems on her husband. Saying he was physically and mentally abusive towards her as well as in front of the children.

While I never had the opportunity to meet him in person, my Aunt Hannah tells me he was indeed a good, kind person. In addition the Court documents and my Mother portrayed him as a violent, mean, man. However, the Courts would not have given him custody of three children if they thought he was a "violent or immoral person".

I can say that I admire the fact that he fought for custody and won. The courts would not have given him three children if they though he was a bad or immoral father. And I have only good things to say about his second wife, Melissa. Anyone who can take on three stepchildren and raise them as her own gets an A+ in my book. God Bless them both for giving those children a home, a fighting chance and a future. My Mother could not and would not have done that.

What I don't understand is why she tried so hard to get custody of only her youngest son, Brian and not her other children. It just doesn't make any sense to try and separate them like that. I guess we may never know. Only more secrets, lies . . .

Marriage number two for Maggie was to my father, Neil Zimmerman whom she "claimed she loved". She took advantage of his position as a police officer, drove him to become an alcoholic, caused him to lose his job, took him for what little he had then divorced him leaving him to drink himself to death.

They were living together and telling everyone they were married long before they actually got married. I was born of the union before they were legally married. Nothing like a bastard child to get things started. Dad was a good, kind, man. After the army, he came home and went to work for the Flint Police Department in Flint, Michigan.

He was very proud of his job and was good at it. He was promoted to Detective in January of 1958. But mom, wanted more and it was that which got her into trouble. Their marriage license states they wed on January 17, 1969 in Clearwater, Florida. According to witnesses and documents, this was to avoid prosecution and prevent one another from being able to testify against the other. I will go into this in more detail later. This marriage ended in January of 1975. Conveniently, after all risk of prosecution was over.

Marriage number three took place on April 02, 1976. That marriage also ended in divorce amid verbal claims that he was drinking too much and would become abusive to her

From where I sat, there was a pattern emerging. Was it greed? Sex? Money? Influence? That drove her to abandon her children, turn on her spouses and leave everything behind? I wasn't sure if I would ever know the answer to those questions, but I felt compelled to at least try to find the answers. Then maybe I could prevent myself from making the same mistakes myself. I didn't want to be, "the apple that doesn't far from the tree

Chapter 3

Daddy

Neil Zimmerman proudly poses in his
police uniform with daughter Diane

My father, Neil Zimmerman, was born December 14, 1926 in Flint, Michigan as Neil William Turek. He was the son of a barber and a homemaker. His parents were Hungarian immigrants. He, and his younger brother, James, grew up Catholic in a typical, strict European household. In December of 1945, dad joined the army and served with the 86th Chemical Mortar Battalion in Camp Campbell, Kentucky and in the Headquarters of the second army, Fort George G. Meade, Maryland.

According to his Army records, he spent four months in basic training, seven months as a rifleman, two months as a switchboard operator, and eleven months as a personnel clerk. He performed a variety of clerical and typing duties in the battalion headquarters such as preparing and typing military correspondence, endorsements, reports and standard forms peculiar to military administrative and personnel matters. He did the filing of reports, records, correspondence and military directives. He also prepared and typed payrolls, insurance and allotment forms. I think this laid the foundation for his life as he was forever keeping track of every penny he spent and every move he made. This lead to his ability to type approximately 55 words per minute, which was not bad for a man with short stubby fingers! (One of the only things my sister and I inherited from him).

It was through the Army that he met his first love, Connie Ann Gruner, who came from Nashville, Tennessee. She was young and beautiful. He and Connie were married December, 01, 1946 in Hopkinsville, Kentucky by a Justice of the Peace. Connie, however, came with her own set of secrets and lies. When she was only 12 years old, she discovered she was pregnant. We're not sure of the exact circumstances as we did not find out about her pregnancy until many years after her death. We do know that the baby, a boy, did not survive. We also know that she married at around the same time, no doubt due to pressure from her family. This was as a result of the pregnancy, which was seen as "the right thing to do back then."

Dad apparently knew nothing of Connie's first marriage or her pregnancy when he married her. In fact, it was not until after they had married and he had taken her to live with his parents that he discovered she had been married and had not gotten a divorce from her first husband. How would he explain this to his parents? For now he wouldn't. Instead, he would return Connie to Tennessee where she would file for the necessary paperwork, in order for their marriage to be legal she had to file for a divorce from her first husband. It would be the beginning of a secret never to be learned of until our Grandmother's death in 2005, when a letter Connie wrote was discovered. When she returned, she would live with Dad's parents until he left the Army in June of 1947 with an Honorable Discharge.

Connie and Dad then moved into a small house on Flint's east side. My sister, Diane, was born of this union on

March 18, 1948. In February of 1949, Dad and Connie had a second child, a baby boy. Unfortunately, that baby died a day later. It was believed that he was born premature. However, I vividly remember a conversation I had with my grandmother regarding the baby. It was her opinion that the baby was not only premature, but she believed, "Connie's foolish drinking and overexerting herself", before the baby was due was the cause for the early delivery. As Grandmother told it, "She moved a whole room of heavy furniture around by herself, thus causing her to prematurely go into labor".

In August of 1950 Dad joined the Flint Police Department. He was very proud to be a police officer and truly enjoyed that type of work. In September of 1957, he legally changed his last name to "Zimmerman" because he felt that the "Turek" name was too hard to pronounce and spell. Yes, here in America, most would find this name would not roll off the tongue. He filed for all of the necessary legal paperwork, but when it came back to him, he noticed that it had an error on it. My sister's name was listed as Marie Diane and it should have been Diane Marie. Instead of making the necessary corrections and waiting for the correct paperwork to return, he wrote the corrections on the document. He considered his personal "correction" legal. It was many years later that we discovered what a problem that was going to be for her. She had tried to get a copy of her birth certificate and was not able because of the way her name appeared. Once again, Dad, in his ultimate wisdom, really messed things up for the rest of us!

In June of 1960, Dad filed for a divorce from Connie.

> The divorce papers taken from the Genesee County Court stated that she broke her marriage vows and was guilty of many acts of extreme cruelty. They also stated that she drank liquor to excess and associated with men other than her husband for reasons that were neither moral nor righteous. She refused to preform regular household duties with any consistency. It was impossible for the two of them to discuss her drinking or refusal to cook without it ending up in a temper tantrums. R4

Her refusal to stop drinking and cooking had caused an estrangement between her and my sister who was then twelve years old. It was getting to the point that my sister did not want to live with her own Mother so Dad was asking for sole custody in the divorce.

Dad would be starting over now with a teenaged daughter. However, he didn't want to cut Connie out of the picture all together, for she was Diane's mother. So with the help of his parents, he would raise Diane.

Needless to say, Connie never did speak of her first marriage or the child she had that died. I cannot image the fear and shame she must have felt when she discovered that she was pregnant at such a young age. And then to be forced into a marriage, "probably because it was seen as the as the right thing to do at that time". Had she been raped? Was the father a family member? A stranger? Or an enlisted man on leave?

Furthermore, according to Tennessee law, the age of consent was considered eighteen. However, one may marry at age sixteen if there were "special circumstances", such as pregnancy. And even younger minors could receive a license to marry at that time. The youngest ages I found while researching this book were in Kansas where males could marry at the age fourteen and females at the age of twelve. Yes, twelve. What does a girl at the age of twelve know about pregnancy or marriage? She is stuck somewhere between childhood and adulthood; still growing, still developing, and still maturing.

If it was in fact an incest issue, here is something else to consider. Twenty-five states prohibit marriages between first cousins. Six states allow first cousin marriage under certain circumstances, and one allows first cousin marriage, but prohibits double-cousin marriage. Most states recognize marriage of first cousins married in a state only where such marriages are legal. Then there may have been the need for a proxy marriage if he was an enlisted man. Try explaining all that to a twelve year old!

One day during a conversation with my sister she said, "If I had only known about all this before", referring to what her mother had gone through as a teenager. "Obviously it would have made a world of difference" while I was growing up. The conversation came about while talking about our grandmother's death. As we were going through her things, my sister found a letter that her mother had written as a teenager. In it she described in detail what she had gone through. "Why didn't Grandma or my Mother ever talk about these things?" She pondered. "People didn't talk about those kind of things back then", I said. "She probably felt Grandma and Grandpa would have somehow thought less of her if they would have known the truth." The tears welling up in my sister's eyes. Unfortunately, there were more questions now than answers. We don't know how Grandma got ahold of that letter or why she even kept it all those years. While I never saw it, I only know of its existence.

My sister, like me, had a rough childhood. Her mother, like mine, was an alcoholic "who liked men and didn't want to cook or clean", according to our father and divorce documents.

It made sense really when you think about it. Dad had the typical rescuer personality. People with this type of personality have a conscious need to help others out of difficult situations. For Dad that meant picking the same type of woman each time he married.

Guilt was a constant way of life for him. He always felt the need to serve or help, whether in the army, on the police department or as a barber. Likewise when rescuers find things not going as planned, high levels of stress show up which lead to additions. In dad's case that meant alcoholism. Dad's compulsive need to help also lead to another "weird secret".

After Dad and Connie divorced, Dad continued to help and see Connie. The weird part was that he began telling everyone that "she was his sister". By this time he was dating my mother, so of course he didn't want her to know who she was. Therefore, he had to keep to secret going. It got ever stranger when Connie was having financial problems and Dad let her move in with them for a short time. My mother never learned Connie's true identity until just before her death in October of 2004. Mom was "shocked" to learn that Connie was not Dad's sister, but in fact his first wife. Why did he feel the need to make this lie up and to continue to keep it going for so long? I too grew up for years going to her farm for visits on Sundays. I always called her "Aunt Connie or just Connie as I got older." I realized one day that my sister had suffered just as I had. She had longed for her Mother's love as a child and teenager, but anger and resentment had gotten in the way. When she finally found what she needed to forgive and understand her, it was too late. My heart felt heavy and I could now feel the tears in my own eyes began to well up. I had went through the same thing with my Mother. We had went for years without speaking. The anger and hatred I felt towards her for so many different things had built like a dam until it finally broke and I confronted her. I too, got nowhere. Only more questions than answers because of so many secrets and lies. The shame was, it didn't have to be that way. We had lost out on that special Mother-Daughter relationship and the years of love and trust that should have gone with it.

Why did my family feel the need to lie when it came to so many things? I was starting to wonder if I would ever learn the truth.

Chapter 4

Man Missing   Information Needed

They say a picture is worth a thousand words . . . this one surely was. It also contained a thousand questions. As I held the newspaper clipping in my hands, I wondered how I would I tell my fiancé about this part of my life. Knowing that it wasn't going to be easy, I looked again at the article, this time focusing on the photo that was with it. The man's dark eyes in the photo seemed to stare back at me, his mouth open as if he wanted to say something, but couldn't. If he could only talk I thought to myself? What would he say? "The newspaper clipping had been passed on to me by my grandma Marie back when I was a teenager. She felt it was important for me to have it since it involved my parents. It was creased, faded, and hard to read. The short article, was taken from the December 04, 1968 edition of The Flint Journal which read as follows:

FLINT MAN MISSING; FOUL PLAY SUSPECTED

The Flint Police believe that there may have been foul play in the disappearance of a Flint man. He was last seen getting into an automobile driven by a woman around noon November 9th, 1968.

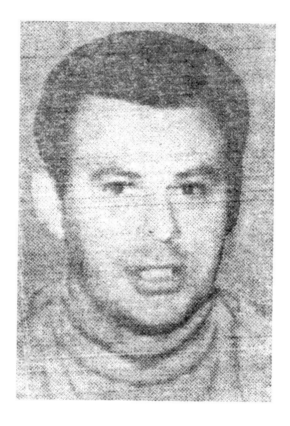

Robert Henry Boileau

Detectives identified him as Robert Henry Boileau, 32 who got into the car after leaving the place where he works, Peoples Outfitting Company, 3316 S Dort Hwy.

Officers said that Boileau had frequently left town on occasions for several days but always kept in telephone contact with friends. No one has heard from him since Nov. 9th. He was reported missing November 13th.

Fellow employees said he left the Peoples store after making a date by phone with a woman, detectives said.

He got into a 1958 white, four door, hardtop Cadillac.

Police have asked anyone who saw such a car on that day or have any information about Boileau's whereabouts to call Detective Sgt. Leo Johnson or Detective Michael Kostka in the detective bureau at the Flint Police Headquarters.

Boileau weighs about 200 pounds and has brown eyes, medium complexion, long hair with pronounced sideburns, a scar through the left eyebrow, a scar on the inside of the left arm and a birth mark on the back of the neck.

When last seen, officers were told he was wearing a white short-sleeved turtleneck shirt, dark blue trousers, a plaid sport coat and a black double breasted topcoat and was carrying about $60. [R5]

Personal photo of Maggie Zimmerman
standing by the 1958 White Cadillac

Along with this article, my grandmother also kept several photographs. One was of my mother standing in front of a 1958 white, four door, hardtop Cadillac. The car, owned by my father, Neil Zimmerman, clearly shows a license plate, which if enlarged, identifies the make and model the police were looking for. Another photo shows my mother, whose hair color was changed from dark to blonde about this time, making her a match to the description in the police report. At one point, I talked with one of the Detectives handling the case. He told me that my mother was considered the prime suspect in the case, and that she had been under surveillance for some time. I found out that they just never could gather enough evidence to pin anything on her. She had been working in a pizzeria restaurant when this good looking wealthy man came in. He wore diamonds, expensive clothes and gave her large cash tips. Before long she was infatuated with him. This intoxication would come with a price though. One that would cost her and two families dearly. According to the police, the deed would require her to start by picking Boileau up at is place of employment. Then as the article states, they believe she was the last person he was seen with when she drove off with him in her car. It's unknown what happened after that, but police speculate that she drove him to where he was to be killed.

It was shortly after Boileau's disappearance that mom took a trip to see her sister, Judy and brother-in-law Frank in Florida.

There at the Airport Judy and her daughter Annie waited for my Mother to arrive. After no one showed up and they thought everyone had departed from the plane, they became worried and headed toward the desk. Just then a beautiful blonde haired woman dressed in a fur coat with diamonds, high heels and expensive clothes, showed up and said, "What's the matter Judy? Aren't you going to say hello to your sister?"

Upon turning around and gazing at her they suddenly realized that it indeed was her. My cousin stood in disbelief thinking to herself, "She looked like a glamourous, movie star!"

During Mom's stay, two FBI agents showed up from the Tampa office to question her about her involvement in the Boileau disappearance. She boldly ascertained her innocence, saying she would not talk to or cooperate with them, and told them just where they could go. Frank, who was in the process of applying for a really good job, was scared spitless that mom had just done something that would screw up his chances to get that job. My aunt and uncle were horrified by her behavior. How could she talk to the authorities in this manner? Didn't she have any manners or respect for authority figures? They were beside themselves. After all, wasn't she was married to a police officer, for heaven's sake! Frank, who was usually an extremely calm and gentle man by nature, was livid! At that moment his family was certain he would kill Maggie if he "lost this opportunity to move up and get the job of his dreams."

My mother returned to Flint shortly after that. The following month my father lost his job with the Flint Police Department. He was a Detective Sargent and had been with the department for eighteen years. It is believed that he was forced to take a deferred retirement because of my mother's involvement in the Boileau disappearance. Dad had tried to smooth things over for her and help her out so that she would not get into trouble, but instead he ended up taking the fall for something she had done. Once again Dad got involved with a woman who he thought he could help, and it back fired on him. Not only did he lose the job he loved because of her, but some of his retirement and benefits he lost as well.

My Mother and Father made a last minute trip to the Pinellas County Court House in Clearwater, Florida. There they were legally married on January 17, 1969 by a Justice of the Peace. This last minute, out-of-state marriage, was believed to be a strategy to protect them from having to testify against one another. For at the time, they were only living together and saying they were married. However, if they legally married, they would be prohibited by the law of, "Spousal privilege", and from testifying against one another.

Interestingly enough, I was with them on this trip. I was four going on five. Yes, that means I was an illegitimate child, born out of wedlock. I remember standing with them in front of the court house as my Grandpa Stiles took our picture. There on the glass door under the word 'Licenses' were the words: *Driving, Hunting, Fishing and Marriage.* My Dad who was dressed in a dark suit stood pointing at the word, "Fishing", with a big grin on his face.

He was always such a joker. Mom stood next to him in a navy suit and I, in front of her, in a light blue, flowered

Neil & Maggie Zimmerman
on their Wedding Day with
I, Isabella, looking on at
Pinellas County Court
House, Clearwater, Florida

Grandfather Phillip, my
Mother and I enjoying
a sunny day at
Clearwater Beach

dress with my hair pulled back in pig tails complete with pretty ribbons. Not really understanding why we were there, I remember a little later sitting in one of the huge wooden court house chairs while they got married. I felt so small in comparison to those chairs. The chair arms seemed to engulf me, and I found my feet swinging back and forth unable to reach the floor. I recall staring endlessly out the window, eager to go outside to the warmth and sunshine of Florida. (It was cold and snowy back home in Flint.) A nice lady, who was watching me while my parents were gone, asked my name, and played a counting game with the cars outside and stated their colors as they zipped by the window. I then told her that we were going to the beach while we were there. She smiled and said that we would enjoy that. It wasn't long after that that my parents returned and we headed out to the beach. It took us only a few minutes to get there, as it was only a few blocks away. I remember my mom taking off my shoes and the feeling of the warm sand between my toes as I ran back and forth squealing in sheer delight. My dad bought a bag of popcorn, and we spent time throwing it up into the air to feed the seagulls. At first, I was scared when so many gulls began to swarm all around me, but when I realized that they were not going to hurt me and it became fun. Thinking back on that day, it all seemed so perfect. I was with my mother, father and Grandpa Stiles in Florida. It was a beautiful, sunny 72 degree day. We were laughing and playing in the sand and water. It all seemed so perfect to me, but in hind sight, it was probably the worst day of their lives. They had flown there to marry and keep from having to testify against one another. Dad had lost his job and a career that meant so much to him and mom, well, she was considered a prime suspect in this murder and kidnapping case. So in hindsight, I guess it wasn't such a perfect day after all.

When my parents returned home to Flint, a grand jury would be convening. It would be just the beginning of a long investigation that would last for many years. During this time period, my parents had decided to invest in an old farm house that was located directly next door to the house they were living in on Flint's south side. The house, which was in need of a lot of repairs, was just what the two of them needed to keep themselves busy. Even turning the upper half of the house into a separate apartment that could be rented out to bring them extra income.

Dad would do the maintenance work and mom would do whatever decorative or cosmetic work needed to be done. They spent all their spare time on the house and in no time at all, it was almost done. Then one night a fire broke out burning the house almost to the ground. While it was never proven, it was believed that my Mother (a heavy chain smoker, who was a regular smokestack), had left a cigarette burning in an area near wood scraps and saw dust. While arson couldn't be proved, it was highly suspected, the plan was to collect the insurance money and rebuild it again. Could my mother have planned this fire which smoldered for hours before bursting into flames just so she could collect the insurance money? (In my opinion, yes!) But things were getting rocky between them and their marriage would last only until January of 1975 when they would file for a divorce.

Nothing like a little conspiracy, kidnapping, murder, and arson to tear a family apart or in this case, keep it together.

NOTE: This is still an open cold case. If you have any information regarding this case, please contact the Author.

All of the reports and supplemental paperwork involved in this case has "mysteriously disappeared" from both the FBI and Flint Police Department. What else would you expect when the Mafia is involved? I personally know that they existed as I saw the FBI reports at one time and spoke with Det. Michael Kostka at another. When I went back at a later date to get copies of them, they were gone. Hmmmmmm . . . guess I should have taken them when I had them in my hot little hands!

Chapter 5

Kindergarten and Elementary Years

In hindsight, I have only a few personal memories of my life with my parents. One of the most vivid was when I six years old. I was leaving school for the day. I had been going to Freeman Elementary School which was only a few blocks from our home. I can still clearly see the front of the school in my mind. At the end of that particular day, while walking home, I held a freshly baked cookie in my left hand that was in the shape of a traffic light. It was complete with red, orange and green circles filled in with colored icing to indicate the different traffic lights. In class we had learned about the traffic signals and what the different colored lights meant. Great subject and clearly a very important one as I passed several traffic lights on my way home each day. The only problem I was really struggling with, was whether to take it home and show my parents or to just eat the darn thing! I felt like I had a devil on one shoulder and an angel on the other, "Go ahead. Just eat it, nobody cares what you did in school today". "No, wait!" Back and forth I pondered! Then I looked around to make sure no one was watching, and I took a really big bite right off of the top! Oh well, too late now, there was no turning back. Only crumbs left of that project. Now what should I do? Chances are no one was going to greet me at the door and ask me what I did today anyway, so it wasn't really going to be a problem. I quickly tossed the final crumbs in my mouth and headed for home.

There's another's incident that very much stands out in my mind. I was about the same age and my mother and I were home alone. I was in the living room watching TV when suddenly she grabbed me from behind. With a finger to her mouth indicating that I was to be quiet, she told me to go hide under my bed until Daddy came home. My dad was my one true hero. I guess I must have not moved fast enough because she gave me a good shove and pointed one more time towards my bedroom. Once more pointing to her mouth and saying in a quiet voice, "Don't make a sound. Understand?" I nodded and stumbled quickly off to the bedroom to scramble under my bed. As I lay quietly under the bed, I heard sirens in the background. I had never seen my mother frightened like this before.

Scared spitless, I looked back, only to see her with a gun in her hand and heading towards the kitchen. It wasn't unusual to see my dad with a gun, but it was my mother. I was super scared now. I didn't want anything bad to happen to her or my dad. As I lay quietly under the bed, with sirens growing louder in the background, I was afraid to look up. With my face buried deep into the carpet, and my hands and arms covering my eyes and ears, this is one time I would do as I was told. I would wait till Daddy came home to tell me it was okay to come out. I know, I told myself, make a game of it. I would pretend I was playing hide and seek. That's it, I was hiding. I must be very quiet so that no one could find me. At about this time, someone came through the door of the bedroom. I saw a pair of shiny black shoes and what I thought was the bottom of my dad's blue uniform. I could feel myself holding my breath, only my eyes moving as the person came closer. Part of me wanted to reach out to the legs, but Mom had said to be quiet and wait. Suddenly, a hand appeared out of nowhere and began moving around under the bed as if it was looking for something. I held my breath. My bed was full-sized and backed against the wall in the corner as far back as it would go. I too was as far back in the corner as I as could go. The hand could not get close to me. I was safe for at least the time being. Then I heard that familiar voice say, "Honey, are you down there?" It was my dad! "Daddy, Daddy", I yelled as I wiggled out from under the bed. "It's you!" With a big sigh, I threw my arms around his neck and jumped up on his knee as he kneeled at the edge of the bed. He lifted me up and carried me into the kitchen where I sat down at the kitchen table. There I sat with Mom, Dad and another officer. Mom went on to tell Dad how we had been watching TV when she heard a man break into the back of the house and try to come up the stairs. She went on to tell them how she had scared him off with a gun. I continued to be scared for some time after that incident, so much so, that I began having nightmares and wetting the bed.

It was shortly after that incident, that I was sent to live with my paternal grandparents, György and Maria Turek. This was Dad's idea as my parents were headed for a divorce and they felt I would have a more stable home environment if I went to live with my grandparents. I also would have the advantage of going to a better, larger school which was close to their house.

My Grandpa György and Grandma Marie were both Hungarian. György, a barber by trade, was born in Sarud, Hungry, a small town outside of Budapest. He had immigrated to the US in 1910 along with his mother, Mary and brothers, Thomas and Giorgi.

Marie, whose maiden name was Szabò, was born in Ohio in 1906. She and Gyòrgy met and went on to marry on January 30, 1926. They later had two children, Neil and James.

Now here's where it gets sticky. By now my parents' divorce was final, and he has me living with his parents with the belief that I would be better off in a two parent family. His other belief was that my being there would keep them from yelling at one another. YES, he actually thought having a child there would keep things peaceful.

He knew they had a habit of fighting with one another and even that things could turn violent. One such example, was retold by my sister, Diane. Grandpa who apparently got so mad, put his fist through the front glass door in a fit of rage. He not only broke the door, but lacerated his hand and really scared the girls. He took off before the police could get there, but they finally caught up with him and took him to Hurley Hospital to get patched up. Because of the rage and outburst, they decided to keep him in the psychiatric unit where he received shock treatments before being released. My sister and Grandma had a "code word" that they used whenever Grandpa got drunk or disorderly. When that word was mentioned, they knew to hide and call Dad and or the police. I found out later that Grandpa had a really rough childhood. According to his nephew's wife, Rose Turek, his father use take a cat-o-nine tail whip, heat it in a fire, then proceed to beat him and his brothers with it. I swear my heart skipped several beats when I heard this. There were times when Grandpa was extremely mean to both Grandma and I. Now I know from where his anger originated. And they felt this was a good place to put a child??????

This home would involve two married people who could provide a more traditional family. One that came complete with love, care, stability, religious beliefs and more. At least that was the plan. But instead I got anger and abuse.

I found out that after Giorgi and Rose married they moved to Seattle, Washington in an attempt to get "as far away from the family" as they could. Thinking that it was the family that was "bad", they went on to start their own family by having sons, Phil and Emil and later then daughter Julia. It is here that the first documentation of mental illness appears in the family. Phil's daughter, Kimberly, battled mental illness much of her life. She died at the young age of 26. Her mother, Autumn, acted as her advocate helping her navigate through the complex mental health system. Then on my mother's side, my Aunt Hanna's daughter Pamela was also diagnosed as being bipolar. None of this helped me though because I didn't find out about it until I started researching my genealogy.

So that left me alone to live with my grandparents, I had to change schools. Not yet finishing kindergarten at Freeman Elementary, I had to continue my classes at the larger Civic Park Elementary School. I thought because it was so close to home, I would be able to walk there. My grandfather, however, would not hear of such a thing! He was very strict and either drove me to school or walked me there. I was so embarrassed by his behavior for many of the other children got to walk to school on their own. "Why did he have to come with me all the time?" I often wondered to myself. He was always watching me like a hawk or hovering over me, and I didn't understand why. Then one day I took my anger out on him with a well-aimed and fully packed snowball which hit him square in the right ear. His face turned red with anger and he came at me with a clenched fist. I quickly dodged his swing and managed to stay several steps ahead of him the rest of the trip home. Needless to say, I was in big trouble when we got home. That was another thing back then, you knew if you got in trouble at school, you could count on getting in even more trouble at home. I remember our gym teacher, a tall black man who had a long paddle with holes in it. He wasn't afraid to use it either. I tried hard to stay out of trouble and under the radar so to speak, but sometimes it just didn't work. I disliked school with a purple passion and it showed. At one point, I wasn't happy with my grades, so I took it upon myself to change them. The teacher gave me my report card to take home and after seeing what she had given me, I went searching for a pen and an eraser. I worked so hard on erasing the grades that there was hardly any paper left to write on. No problem. I just wrote in what I thought I should have gotten. I might have gotten away with it if it hadn't been for the fact that your parents or guardian had to sign it. The signed card was then returned for the teacher to mark your next quarter's grade. When my teacher saw the grades had been tampered with, a call went home and guess who was in trouble again? Then there was the time that I made up the story about John hitting me. He was a nice enough kid, complete with big blue eyes and long, shaggy blonde hair, but for some reason, I had it out for him. I decided to make up "a story" and tell my grandparents that John had hit me at school. Well, that lie got me attention alright. My Grandparents contacted the school and John's parents. Soon I was getting lots of attention. It just wasn't the kind I had hoped for!

There is another day that stands out in my memory that I am sure I will never forget. It was Saturday, March 18, 1972. It was my sister's birthday. But that wasn't why I was so excited. That afternoon Civic Park School caught fire and was nearly destroyed. We saw the huge plumes of black smoke from home. Not knowing what was on fire at first, we followed the smoke only to discover that indeed my elementary school was ablaze. We stood across the street and watched in awe as the big black clouds billowed up into the sky. I remember thinking silently and then aloud, "Does this mean I don't have to go to school?" With a touch of excitement in my voice I looked at the others who had also gathered to now watch. Many I recognized as classmates. My mind was racing with only one thought, "No school, hurray!" That freedom didn't last long though. We were all sent to surrounding schools to finish our educations until Civic Park could be rebuilt and reopened the following December. I was sent to the nearby St. Luke's Catholic Church School which I was already familiar with since we went to church there. It was close by and the classes were small.

I was never what you would call a "happy child". I was socially isolated, withdrawn and awkward and made only a few friends no thanks to my grandparents. In fact, they worked hard at keeping kids away. There were three young children close to my age that lived next door that were labeled as "bad" by my grandfather very early on. Their mother, who was the only parent in the household, was in and out of jail and choose to "entertain different men" on a regular basis. I took a liking to the oldest child, Henry, who was a real trouble maker. He was consistently throwing eggs at our house, walking on the grass when Grandpa told him not to, and writing all over our sidewalk with his brightly colored chalk. He really knew how to "push Grandpa's buttons" so to speak, and most of the time it seemed to be over harmless things. After all, what was so bad about walking on the grass or coloring on the sidewalk? According to grandpa he was going to go to Hell for sure. I can still see my grandpa hiding behind the blinds in Grandma's bedroom, peering out for what seemed like hours and swearing over and over again in Hungarian at poor little Henry. Once I began to like and get along with Henry, Grandpa laid down the "Rules". I was told to "never go inside their house or their garage". I often wondered why, but never was given a reason and knew better than to ask for one. Shortly after that, playing with him or his siblings was off limits all together. Unfortunately, my only contact with Henry after that was watching him from behind the blinds as well.

Another friend of mine was Adam, who lived just down the street from us. His father was on the same police department as my dad. Adam had two brothers. Since I was sort of a tomboy, I got along well with his brothers who were close to our age. We often played cops and robbers and rode our bikes up and down the street. I wasn't allowed to go far and only where my grandparents could see me. I always had to be in early, usually by 5:00 pm, unlike the other kids who could stay out until dark. I never quite understood why they were so protective of me. It wasn't long before the kids didn't want to play with me because of my grandparents' strict rules. They wanted to ride, run and play and so did I, for that matter, but Grandpa was always looking out the window at us. He yelled if we ran on the grass, were too loud or did anything that he didn't approve, which seemed to be just about everything.

My other friend was a young girl of my age named, Theresa. Theresa was my only female friend, so I really treasured "our time together". She had an older sister who, of course, Grandpa didn't approve. I don't exactly know why. But he seemed to approve of Theresa and he would often let her come over and stay awhile as long as her sister was not with her. Sometimes he would even take us ice skating which we loved to do. Our favorite ice skating spot was Ballenger Park. However, if we couldn't go there and the weather permitted, we would sometimes skate on the street in front of my house. (Those of you that are from Michigan know that the streets get icy more than we would like, but we kids loved it. It usually meant a snow day from school and our own personal ice skating rink. What more could a kid ask for?)

That aside, I have to admit Grandpa had some really dumb rules. Who I could play with? How I could play with them? How late I could stay up? Whether I could go outside or not? It seemed that being a child or having fun just wasn't something he believed in. Was this the way he had been brought up? Were his parents like this with him?

I often wondered what his parents and childhood must have been like. It wasn't until the researching of this book that I found out the answer of those questions. Then, suddenly the way he treated me as a child, and even an adult, all suddenly made sense.

Kindergarten classes were held in the basement of the Civic Park Elementary school. Our teacher was a beautiful lady with long, dark hair that she always keep up in a tight bun. One day, shortly after I arrived, we all sat in a large circle on the floor. Each child took a turn and introduced themselves by name and said a little about their parents. I stiffened up and my throat got tight. What on earth was I going to say? My last name was different and I didn't know how to explain why I was living with my grandparents instead of my parents. This was not going to be easy. Maybe I could say I had to go to the bathroom. I tried to think of a way out of this, but I just couldn't think fast enough. Before I knew it, it was my turn and everyone was staring at me. "Good Lord, now what do I do?" I cleared my throat, looked down at the floor and mumbled my name as quietly as I could. "Speak up, dear child", the teacher said. "What is your name?" This was definitely not going well. "Bella. But, my real name is Isabella, Isabella Rothbury and I live with my grandparents. Right away a child yell out. "Where are your parents?" Kids, can be so cruel. I looked right at him as I said, "My dad is a policeman." I couldn't have been any prouder. Then another child next to me spouted off, "Where's your mother? How come you don't live with them?" I could feel everyone's eyes on me, watching and waiting for an answer. Strangely enough. I wanted an answer to that question too.

"W E L L", I said, "My dad and mom work long hours, so I live with my grandparents during the week and see my parents on the weekend". It sounded like a good answer, but I could see that several kids were thinking about what I had just said. They probably had parents who worked as well and still got to live at home, so why wasn't I? I think our teacher finally saw how horribly uncomfortable I was becoming and quickly moved on to the next child. "Whew", I thought, "glad that's over." There was another day in kindergarten where we were learning how to brush our teeth; something most of the other children were already familiar with it. I however, was not because my grandparents were from the old county and they just didn't do many of the routine things that were normally done here in America on a regular basis. Again, the teacher had to show me how to do this simple task that the others did and seemed to know all about. I felt their eyes on me as she showed me how to make the simple up and down brush strokes on my teeth. This was happening far too often for my liking and I remember thinking to myself,

"Why is this happening to me? Why am I the only one who doesn't know how to do these things?"

I not only wasn't finding any answers, but things were about to get worse. For as far back as I can recollect, I remember feeling "uncomfortable" with a number of things during the years that followed. These events felt wrong to me as a child and now as an adult I know that they were. One such example was the location of my bed. It was placed in Grandpa's room. I'm not sure why you would put a seven year old in the same room with a grown man, but that's how it started. Initially there were separate beds, but both of us were in the same room.

Grandma on the other hand, had her own room with a full sized bed all to herself. Why did they not share a room like most husband and wives? Why not switch rooms? Shouldn't the girls have been together? I can even see putting the girls together in the larger bed if necessary. As I got older, I became more and more depressed and withdrawn. Bath time was another awkward and uncomfortable situation. In fact, I considered it a good reason to hide. First Grandpa would take a bath, then Grandma, and then I. By then, the water was dirty and there was a dark, grayish scum across the top. The water temperature would be cool if not cold by this time. Sometimes Grandma and I would take a bath together. There was one time that the water was so cold that she decided to try and add some more to it. Grandma and I sang loudly and splashed in the water while she tried to add a little extra to it. While it didn't bother me to bathe with Grandma, it did when Grandpa wanted me to. Even as a child I knew something wasn't right. It just didn't feel appropriate. He would start out with a little bubble bath and suds up the water. Then have me sit on the edge of the tub. Sometimes he would hand me a sudsy rag and ask me to "scrub his back". Another thing that made me uncomfortable was when I had to use the bathroom and he would be taking a bath. Since we only had the one bathroom, I would hold it as long as I could. But he would purposely stay in there longer refusing to cover himself or pull the curtain when I entered. Talk about making a person "feel dirty".

I wanted so much to be near someone, but didn't want to be touched. I was so confused by what was going on. I felt like scrubbing and cleaning my skin until it peeled off, but bathroom time was precious and limited. There was no such thing as privacy. We weren't allowed to spend much time in the bathroom and water was rationed. I would go to Grandma's room whenever I got scared. She would quiet me and take me back to my bed. Grandma would usually let me sleep with her for a few days and "the cycle" would start all over again. Her weight would cause the bed to sag towards the center, and I would find myself desperately clinging to the sides until I fell asleep. I would go through periods of sleepwalking, having nightmares and even bed wetting.

I later discovered that this was actually a fairly harmless and common occurrence among children which starts within an hour or so of going to bed. Each episode can range from 5 to 15 minutes and while most children tend to outgrow it, however you do need to safeguard them from injury while they are sleepwalking and try to determine what the root cause of the problem is. Some of the more common causes are:

- fatigue or lack of sleep
- irregular sleeping habits
- stress or anxiety
- being in a different sleep environment
- illness or fever
- certain medications, including sedatives, stimulants, and antihistamines
- genetic factors (a family history of sleepwalking)

In addition to walking, there are other actions which are associated with sleepwalking.

- sitting up in bed and repeating motions
- getting up and walking around the house
- talking or mumbling during sleep
- not responding when spoken to
- making clumsy movements
- urinating in inappropriate places
- performing routine or repetitive behaviors, such as opening and closing doors [R6]

In my case I had a number of these. For example, I usually ended up in Grandma's closet either in a fetal position or trying to urinate. I also walked about the house mumbling, trying to open and close things. I often had night terrors along with an occasional nightmares. (Nightmares are dreams with vivid and disturbing content that the child remembers vs Night terrors where the child cannot be awakened and normally doesn't remember anything. It usually takes place in combination with sleepwalking.) During my sleepwalking episodes, Grandma would take me and gently guide me back to her bed. I shared a room with Grandpa until I was in my teens. He always wore this knee length night gown that Grandma made special for him at Christmas. She spent endless hours sewing in the basement. (Now I realize that it was her way of getting away and escaping.) While I loathed the sound of his breathing, snoring brought a welcome reprieve. Strange as it seems, because then I knew I was "safe". The door to our bedroom squeaked when you tried to open it. However, I literally learned how to very slowly inch it open just enough to get through so that he could not hear it. That way if he woke up and looked at it, it would look like it was still closed. As soon as I heard him snoring, I knew I was safe for the moment. I would get up as quietly as possible and try to open the door without waking him. Then it was a straight shot to safety across the hall to Grandma's bedroom. It took years for me to understand why they slept separately. When I finally asked, Grandma told me, "That his tossing, turning and snoring kept her awake". I was also told that her small TV, which she fought to keep in her room, was keeping him awake.

I have tried, over and over, to write in more detail about the sexual abuse that took place during those years, but I just found it too difficult. Even after years of counseling it still affects my daily life and relationships. Again it's not so much the details of my abuse that are important, but the fact that it sexual assault, abuse or the exposing of oneself, **IS A CRIME**. If you know of or suspect something, <u>please</u> report it to the proper authorities!

It has taken me many, many years of therapy to get to this point and I'm speaking out now because I finally feel I can. I was clearly raped and abused, and as I look back on those years, it is clear that there were obvious "signs or symptoms" that were overlooked. For example, I was not doing well in school, I had attachment issues, was overly passive, withdrawn, was fearful of certain situations, as well as a "specific person", in this case, it was my grandfather. My sleeping patterns changed to include sleep walking, bed wetting, nightmares as well as night terrors. I also started showing anxiety, excessive worrying, frequent complaints stomach aches, headaches, itching and reoccurring infections in the genital area (Which were documented with numerous trips to our family doctor.) Then there was the increased knowledge of or interest in sexual behaviors that were not age appropriate, low self-esteem and feelings of shame and guilt and depression at an early age. In my case, I also ended up repressing memories which was a natural defense mechanism that humans develop to protect themselves from psychological damage. It is usually referred to as "dissociative amnesia". It is the brains way of shutting down and protecting itself from emotional and/or physical violence, sexual abuse and other traumatic events. All of which helps a person cope by allowing them to temporarily (or sometimes permanently) forget the details of an event. This comes about when a person suppresses memories of a traumatic event until they are ready to handle it. Recovery from such a traumatic event can take weeks or months. If you are suffering symptoms that make you believe you might need help, take that important first step and ask a professional for help. Start with you doctor. He or she can at least get you started in the right direction.

Again, I can't reiterate the importance of speaking up if you think, feel or suspect that someone you know has been raped or abused. Across the world millions deal daily with the secrets of rape, child molestation, incest, sexual assault or pornography. Whether it's to report it or give support to someone that went through it many, many years ago. The weight of carrying such a secret **can,** and **does** kill. Please, stand up and do the right thing instead of looking the other way. If you know or suspect something is or has happened . . . do the right thing. Help is only a phone call away. You will be glad you did it in the long run.

Chapter 6

Good Neighbors

Me, standing in front of my neighbor's
beautiful, climbing, red roses

I grew up on Flint's North West side where I lived in a
small, five roomed, white house with yellow trim.
Nothing fancy by any means. It was an averaged size, two
bedroom home with a closed-in back porch. That porch
was reminiscent of many good hours on the swing with
Grandma. The majority of the room consisted of screened
in windows, but the wall where it attached to the house

60

and under the windows was covered in knotty pine. The room was always a bright, favorite location to gather and relax. But my favorite thing to do was to sit was on the swing with Grandma. The backyard was fenced in and shaded by two, large trees. The fence that separated us from our neighbor to the west, was interlaced with the most beautiful, red climbing roses. I can remember as a young child, having my picture taken in front of it. What a spectacular backdrop it made with those bright red, climbing blossoms, and the smell! Mrs. Whipple, who was our neighbor, tended to those roses daily. There was no denying that she **knew** how to grow roses. I was holding my favorite doll, Chrissy who was 18″ tall with beautiful, auburn hair. What I liked best, though, was that she had another adjustable thick lock of hair that came out of her head giving me the ability to adjust the lengths of her hair. I would comb and play with her hair for what seemed like hours. But, I picked this photo to not only to show how beautiful her roses were, but to show how "unhappy or sad" I looked. Literally every photo of me taken during my childhood years shows me with the same "unhappy or sad look" on my face. Could this have been a sign that once again was missed by everyone????

Since playing with the neighborhood children was practically forbidden, I turned to the senior citizens for companionship. There were a good many in our neighborhood, and I seemed to have a real ability to get along with them. I think it had to do with the fact that I had been raised by my grandparents, consequently I was a little more mature for my age than the average child. I always wanted an excuse to get out of the house, and these kind, older folks seemed to really like me chatting with them and being a good listener. Often times they needed help around the house or yard and I was more than happy to lend a hand. I started cutting grass, raking leaves, weeding flower beds and gardens, and even cleaning houses. Soon I was building friendships, making money, and getting out of the house, and learning some really valuable life skills.

Across the street I had Mr. and Mrs. Penley. They never had children of their own, and I think in some ways I was kind of a daughter to them. He worked for General Motors and she was a teacher at Civic Park Elementary School. He loved to garden and was the first to teach me about growing vegetables. He used to have a pretty good sized garden on one side of his garage. A real treat for me was on several occasions we would make Saturday trips to Frankenmuth, Michigan for their famous chicken dinners. Afterwards we would walk through town and look through the shop windows. Whenever I had a problem with my homework I always knew I could go to them and they would help me.

Mary lived down the street on the corner. She had such a love for flowers. I can still see her yard with its beautiful daises, roses and landscaping. She spent a lot of time out there working on it and it showed. She used to have the most beautiful beds of daises. She taught me a lot about caring for flowers. Must be where I got my love for them because anyone who knows me, knows that I would rather have daisies than roses any day. After working on her yard we would often go to the mall and walk around or just sit and watch the people. It was those "close friendships" that I developed with our elderly neighbors that I truly treasured, as they were the friends I should have had, but couldn't.

Behind us lived Mr. & Mrs. Wruck. They were a delightful old couple. You could always find them out in their little back yard doing something. And it showed. They had beautiful flowers and even some vegetables along the garage. They taught me a love for growing veggies so I too grew a small garden behind our garage. Mr. Wruck would often sit in his chair near the back door when he grew tired. Grandma and Mrs. Wruck would meet at the back fence and solve all the world's problems. It was true what they said about fences and friends. Even though there was a fence between our yard and theirs, there was a gate in our neighbor's yard behind their garage that we often used. It was still shorter than walking all around the block.

Our garage had a carport on one side that Grandpa had added on to store his camper trailer when it was not in use.

Grandpa loved to go camping, hunting and fishing, but Grandma wasn't into it so much, and often stayed home. Grandpa would load myself and my Uncle James kids up and together we would travel around to some of Michigan's greatest vacation spots. He even bought a Honda motorcycle at one point. He was in his 60's by then. I remember him buying the plywood and building a large wooden box which he ultimately painted bright orange to place on the back of the motorcycle. This was to not only insure that other people saw him when on the road, but also to give his some storage capability for short runs to the store, or for carrying his barber equipment when he went to cut hair. Grandma and I were so embarrassed over his "orange box", but he insisted on keeping it anyway. It was just big enough to hold two large grocery bags from the store. What's worse is our helmets were that same awful orange color. After all these years, I still can't get that awful shade of orange out of my head.

Chapter 7

Middle School

I went to Donovan North, (Dukette Middle School as it was called back then), and it was a little more challenging for me. It was a tight knit, Roman Catholic school where we learned family values and respect along with math and english. I had to take the bus, which was not far from my home. My grandparents made sure I personally got a ride to the bus stop each day. I again was never allowed to mingle with the other kids. Middle school seemed to be where the crucial change took place. I was fortunate to have two really good teachers that I liked, who took an interest in me and saw to it that I did my homework on a regular basis. It was then that my grades improved.

I was a loner for sure, even though I was surrounded each day in my classrooms with other children. It was as if I were the only one there. My classmates and I played, interacted and even communicated with each other in ways that seemed foreign to me. I felt like I was in a different world and now, as I look back on it, I clearly was.

I felt isolated and alone. I actually worked hard at not interacting with the other kids because I was not like them. I didn't want to explain my differences, for I had learned in elementary school just how cruel kids could be.

I recall a horrifying day between classes when I went to my locker. There was a handwritten note that had been shoved into the slots at the top which read, "You stink". I looked around sheepishly, but the hall was filled with kids and there was no way to figure out which one had delivered the note, so I shoved it into a book and continued on to class. I spent the rest of the day trying to figure out what the note meant. I said nothing to my grandparents when I got home. But the next day at my locker I again found another note similar to the first. Only this one said, "You smell really bad". I took the note along with the other one and went to my teacher, Mr. Davison.

He was a tall man with curly hair who had always been kind to me. Maybe he could help. He read the two notes carefully and placed them on the table in front of us before looking up, and saying as seriously as he could, "Bella, I think they are trying to tell you that they don't like your deodorant". I was almost in tears at this point.

"Deodorant? What is that?" I inquired. I could tell he was trying hard not laugh, but a smile came over his face anyway. "I think we've just figured out what this is all about", he said. So there we sat in his room as he patiently explained how one's body changes and you need something called deodorant. He ended the conversation with, "Do you want me to call your grandparents and talk to them?" "Oh! Good Lord, no! Please don't, I blurted out. I will talk to my grandmother when I get home."

And so I went through the rest of the day, and the bus trip home, trying to figure out how I was going to bring up this subject with her. I had never heard of deodorant and had certainly never seen it in our house. Maybe she knew about it and had it hidden somewhere? This was going to be a long day and night I could tell.

After arriving home, I tried to find a good time to talk to Grandma when Grandpa wasn't around. I told her about the notes the kids had written and the conversation with my teacher. She listened patiently and then finally said, "Those rotten kids". I finally asked her if we had any deodorant and she said no that we didn't use it. Now I was confused. Didn't their bodies change like my teacher said? I was almost panic stricken as I said, "But I can't go back there unless I have deodorant!" My grandmother said, I will talk to your grandfather and we will see what we can do.

So there I sat on pins and needles. I knew this wasn't going to go well. It never did. He was a very stubborn, old fashioned Hungarian. Later that night, Grandma and I approached him as he was reading the newspaper. He peered over the paper just long enough to hear what Grandma said. "She doesn't need deodorant. She smells fine!" he said. "But Grandpa, the kids are calling me bad names. They say I smell, that I stink!" I exclaimed. There was no response from him. We both knew that meant this conversion was over. "Then I won't go to school," I said as I stomped out of the room in tears.

Grandma came in after me and tried to calm me down. "I'll work on him and we'll get you some deodorant sweetheart, don't worry about it. I'll take care it.

But, I was still worried. There was precious little time left before tomorrow morning when school would start. Well, I had to wait a couple days before Grandpa finally broke down and provided me with that *immortalized* deodorant.

As a young woman I struggled to understand my feelings and the changes my body was going through. Those that I did dare to talk about, I was quickly chastised for, especially by my grandfather. It was hard growing up with my grandparents as they were so much older than me.

I felt like they did not want to see or hear a child around. Consequently I was forced to grow up very quickly, not only as a child, but as an adult in a child's body.

Another example, was when I first started my periods. I was thirteen at the time and literally thought I was dying. No one had explained to me that this was "normal" or that it was even going to happen in the first place. I quickly called Grandma into the bathroom to ask her what I should do. She just smiled and said, "You are not dying honey, you are just becoming a woman." Still not quite sure what she meant, I said, "What do I do?" "You'll have to have Grandpa go to the store and get some pads for you", she said. Already I wasn't liking the sounds of this, but I went out to the living room where he was and asked if he could go to the store for me. "What do you need?" he asked. I decided to bring Grandma into this thinking I might have a better chance. Grandma says I've started my period and I need some pads. "You don't need those. Just use toilet paper", he said.

Well, I may not have been actually dying at that point, but I sure wished I was! How could he *SAY* such a thing to me! I ended up storming off to the bedroom in tears. All I could do was pray that Grandma, who had stayed behind, would have better luck convincing him than I did. I could hear her pleading with him as I sobbed. "She's a young woman! You can't expect her to go around stuffing her underpants with toilet paper for Christ's sake! Maybe that's what they did in the olden days, but they don't do that anymore. They make pads these days just for that reason you know."

There was an ice cold silence in the room. One we both knew the meaning of . . . this conversation was over. The next morning, I cried and told Grandma that I wasn't going to school with toilet paper in my underwear. She wiped away my tears and said, "Now you go ahead and go to school and when you get home there will be some pads here for you, okay? Don't you worry about anything. I'll take care of it." In the meantime, I went off to school with several layers of toilet paper stuffed inside my

69

underpants. My pants must have looked like balloons with all the extra padding in them. I was embarrassed beyond belief and convinced that everyone could see it.

Once at school though, I bravely asked a female classmate if she had started her period yet. "Yes" she answered. "Do you have any extra pads with you?" I asked. "Yes, I do. I keep some extra ones in my locker." "May I please get a couple from you?" "Sure", she said. "Never know when you might need them, right?"

"Thanks," I said. "If she only knew", I thought to myself. I should have known more about what was physically happening to me and on top of that I was deeply embarrassed by the situation. I didn't want her or anyone else to know anything about what had happened the night before. People just wouldn't understand and likewise if it got back to Grandpa that I had said something, I would be in big trouble. It was just a no-win situation no matter what I did.

Not long after that, I was practicing one Saturday morning with the church choir for an upcoming holiday. Grandpa showed up for no apparent reason. I got scared as I thought maybe something dreadful had happened at home. But no, instead, he said, "I have come to check up on you." I was so scared of him that I was literally shaking when he left. Several of the adult choir members were concerned for me and asked me if he was always like that?

I was so embarrassed and appalled by this behavior that I broke down and cried when he left. I swore that this had to stop, even if it meant my running away.

I just couldn't take his controlling, manipulative behavior anymore. It seemed to be getting worse. He would say such terribly mean, spiteful things to me. I felt like I was suffocating and I would catch myself constantly looking over my shoulder to see if he was there. I was also fearful of him when he drank a lot or lost his temper. We never knew what was going to set him off, which made it even harder to deal with or even anticipate his mood swings.

On a lighter note, television was seen as a luxury in our home. We had one large one in our living room and another smaller one in Grandma's bedroom. When grandma decided that she wanted to get the smaller TV for her bedroom, you would have thought she asked him to cut off his leg or something. We were not allowed to watch either of them though, unless he gave us permission. With regards to her small TV, a fight ensued about why she didn't need it, how it would cost more electricity to operate and how it would be bad for our eyes. Eventually, after weeks of imploring, she finally got her TV. However, if there was a show that he wanted to see, you can bet he was sitting in front of it and there had better be no interruptions until the end of the program. He usually liked to watch "war or history shows". Those he said were, "good for you, the rest was junk". He might have had a point there?? We would wait till he went to bed then sneak into her room where we would watch a show until we couldn't keep our eyes open any longer or it was over, whichever came first. Then I would tiptoe back into my bed in his bedroom.

What I now realize in my adult years, was that Grandma and I were actually in an abusive relationship with him. We were fearful of Grandpa and constantly walking on eggshells, because he kept us "on a leash" in everything we did. He controlled where we went, the finances, the car, when we slept, when we ate, and on and on.

I knew I couldn't take it much longer. I was like a ticking time bomb about to explode. The question was how longer before it went off?

Chapter 8

High School

High school came with its own set of problems. For example, I was not allowed to take Drivers Education classes because my grandfather felt that I didn't need to learn how to drive, or to even have a license for that matter. He had purchased a four door, burnt orange Cadillac Seville and didn't want anyone else driving it. What was with that color? I was devastated when it came time to sign up for Drivers Education classes. I just didn't understand how he could do this to me. After all, this was America, or so I thought anyway. As I went to church choir practice that week, I was still upset. My friends wanted to know what was wrong, so I told them. One of my dearest friends there was an elderly man named, Walter. He had lost his wife many years earlier and had been a member of the church and choir for many years. Walter was horrified by my grandfather's decision, but quickly had an idea. "How about I teach you how to drive?" He would let me use his car, and we could go out after school and on weekends, and he would give me personized lessons. He would also let me use his car for the test. I was elated! Here was someone who truly believed in me and wanted me to do well. But how could I get my grandparents to go along with it? My

Grandmother had never learned how to drive and had really regretted it all of her life. Maybe I could get her to help me talk Grandpa into it. I knew this wasn't going to be easy. And I was right. It wasn't!

I had not even got the whole sentence out when Grandpa cut me off. "NO, absolutely not!" he exclaimed. "You will not go with him." "Why not?" I asked. "You don't need to learn how to drive!" "Yes, I do!" "And if you won't let me, I'll run away." With that, I ran into the bedroom slamming the door behind me. I headed for my closet. Whenever I was scared or didn't know what else to do, I headed for the safety and security of my closet. There in the darkness I sat and sobbed. Even though the room was dark and small, I knew every inch of it like the back of my hand, with or without the lights on. I had to step up one step to get into it. There in front of me and to the left side was a bench made of wood on which I could sit. To the right, was a rack on which ties could be displayed or hung. Directly in front was a rod on which clothes were hung from hangers.

"How can he do this me and get away with it I wondered? I've got to get out of here. I just can't take this anymore." It was getting to be too much and I couldn't handle it anymore. He wanted to control and manipulate *everything* we said and did. I felt like I was at my breaking point.

There was a light in the closet. Sometimes I would take a book in there a read for a while. At other times I would just silently say my prayers, hoping that God was really there and that he would hear the prayers of this one small, insignificant child. As my mind raced in fear of what I would do if something really bad happened, I had decided that I would go into the closet and go up into the attic through a pull-down door in the ceiling of my closet. There I would be safe. Grandpa would never think to look for me up there. He had told me many times to never, ever go up in that place.

Another issue that came up during my teenage years was that of sex education classes. They were offered at school, but my grandfather wanted to have me excluded. At first, I did not understand why he was so vehemently against me going. I thought it was something really bad or maybe his strict overbearing nature. Then one day one of my school counselors pulled me aside and began to question me. When he realized that I was not going to any activities, class trips, etc. this lead to a call home to my grandparents. Grandpa told him that I didn't need to go to any of those activities and that was the end of that. The counselor finally got him to agree to let me go to the sex education classes, but anything else was out of the question. There would be no dances, no class trips, no prom, no football games, absolutely nothing but basic core classes. His reasoning, he told the counselor was because, "I don't want her around boys". Now I was really confused. I decided to take a trip to the public library and sneak back to the adult section. There I found, "The Joy of Sex" Book which I carefully took off the shelf and began to browse though. It was full of "interesting" pictures. I quickly realized though that there wasn't anything to fear here. After all, I was already familiar with the male body (his), so what was the problem?

With no other outlets, I threw myself into our Church. I was now the choir secretary and had also trained to be a lay reader for the weekend services. (For those of you not familiar with the Catholic Church, this is someone who is responsible for reading aloud excerpts from the Bible at any of the liturgies.) At first, my Grandparents were so proud of me when they saw me in my choir robe and up at the lectern reading. But when I began to spend so much time there, it suddenly became a "problem" for them, especially for my grandfather. I was so thrilled to have something that I enjoyed doing and was good at. So naturally, I threw myself into it with even more time and passion. As you can imagine, that disturbed my Grandfather even more. However, it didn't stop there, as time went on and I got older, I became more aware of many other prejudices, discriminations and negative attitudes that he had. Even though I had been raised in a "Catholic environment", I had a hard time dealing with Grandpa's beliefs and issues. One such example was his homophobia.

As I mentioned earlier, I loved to sing. For six years I sang my heart and soul out and truly loved it! At one point I also became choir secretary. Our group consisted of a fun loving bunch that loved to sing and really got along well together. Soon I felt important and useful for the first time in my life. As I got to know each of them personally, I soon discovered that several of them were either gay or lesbian. While that didn't bother me, Grandpa was furious and wanted me to drop out of the choir immediately. When I refused, a huge fight ensued. As usual, he would not discuss why I should do this, just that I should. Finally at one point, he said that I was getting "too religious", whatever that meant. Grandma finally told me the truth . . . . he didn't want me around "those type of people" anymore. What did he think, that they would turn me into a lesbian? The truth was I needed an escape, and the choir was it. I couldn't have asked for, or had a safer place to go, and I wasn't about to give it up. I felt comfortable and safe around my friends, which is more than I could say of at home. How dare he judge them after all he had done to grandma and me?

I knew how the church and my grandfather felt when it came to homosexuality, but I didn't see it as wrong. It really stirred up a lot of emotion and mixed feelings in me. This was not the only topic we didn't see eye to eye on.

My grandfather spent so much time trying to "shelter me" from bad kids, drugs, alcohol, evil and men that it caused me to lose out on valuable life skills and experiences. The truth was I grew up a bit different than most other children. It was weird, I wanted his love and attention, but not the way he was giving it. I know now he was incapable of giving love to me or Grandma. I so longed for that sense of family and never found it with them or my parents.

There was a great lack of empathy, understanding and sensitivity in our family. There was no denial that Grandpa was in charge. His unequal or unfair treatment of us lead to daily conflict stemming from older immigrant parents that could not cope with changing times or a different culture. We often found ourselves "walking on eggshells" to avoid his furious outburst. It was bad enough that I didn't have a childhood, but I lost out on my teen years as well. Looking back, I see now how I lost out on so many valuable life skills and experiences as well. Many of which would have been helpful in my first marriage.

Chapter 9

Black Sheep #2

I had decided that I wanted to go to college. My grandfather and father wanted me to take business classes. I, however, wanted to go into Law Enforcement. Since both of them were so against that, I ended up enrolling at a local business college. I managed to make it through the first month of classes, but just barely. Then one day, I realized that once again I was forcing myself to do something I did not want to do. As usual, it was what someone else wanted. I was becoming more and more depressed. With each passing day, I became more overwhelmed, and felt myself not wanting to go to class or work. I found it hard to concentrate, had trouble sleeping, low self-esteem and a loss of appetite. It was like the weight of the world was on my shoulders.

Soon I had begun to think that suicide was going to be my only way out. Yet a part of me would say, "You're Catholic, you can't do that. You need to get help." But the question remained, where would I go for that help? I had tried in the past by going to our family doctor. But that did no good. His solution was to put me on birth control pills. Supposedly the pills would regulate my periods and help with the depression. It was a good idea, however, it actually made matters worse. Creating a monster of sorts.

Basically giving a 17 year old with raging hormones free rein on all men. I had now learned that men were interested in me. For once I was in control. At least I thought I was.

I began to party, drink heavily, abuse sleeping pills and have casual, (and many times risky sex) with whomever I wanted. All in an attempt to fill the emptiness within me. After all, I had no intention of ever marrying and I definitely never wanted children. As far as I was concerned, there was no stopping me.

I continued having trouble with my memory. Something both emotional and psychological trauma can affect. I had a large chuck of years (approximately 10 years) during my childhood that was missing or sketchy at best. My doctors said it was a form of amnesia probably caused from childhood trauma. We knew that I had been abused and I always suspected that I may have seen or heard something with regards to the kidnapping and murder of Robert Boileau. That was one of my reasons for undergoing a Sodium Pentothal Interview in November of 1994 in Cincinnati, Ohio (explained in more detail in Chapter 12).

One day while I was in high school, I went to one of my teachers. She taught English and was one of the few people I felt I could trust at the time. I could talk to her about anything at any time. She was the one person that I knew I could always count on no matter what. After listening to me, she suggested that I try to find a good psychiatrist who might be able to better help me. I began a search for someone later that day.

I decided since I had been raised Catholic, that I would begin by talking to our parish priest. However, I felt uncomfortable doing so as I knew he was dealing with issues of his own. He was known throughout the congregation to have a drinking problem and could usually be found at the corner bar with a beer in front of him. He would usually be dressed in blue jeans and a brightly colored floral shirt which made him kind of hard to miss. What bothered me the most, was that the church not only knew about his "problem or secret", but were doing very little about it. Maybe there was more going on behind the scenes that we were not aware of, but it looked like they did more to "hide it" then to try and help him. While he wanted and desperately needed help, somehow he never seemed to get the right kind of help or as much of it as he needed.

One day I spotted him in the parking lot near the rectory. He was standing next to a brand new, shiny, light blue, four door Lincoln Continental Town car. "What do you think of my new car," he asked? "You're kidding, right?" I said as I walked around it eyeing the luxurious exterior. "What? You think I should have got a two door?" he said with a wicked smile. "Well, they will certainly see you coming," I said, shaking my head back and forth. "Yeah, the women are going to love me", he said with a wave of the hand. "What's not to love", I thought? "It looks like a pimp mobile! By the way, don't you think people are going to wonder where you got the money for this?" I said as I stuck my head inside to admire the interior. "I paid for it with my own money!" he said sharply as he got in, slammed the door and started the engine. "I didn't know priests were so well paid," I mumbled under my breath. "Wait till the congregation hears about this", I said. With a final waive of the hand and a honk of the horn he was gone and heading straight towards the corner bar. "Guess this isn't a good time to talk about my problems", I thought. Besides, how could he, a man of the cloth who had problems of his own, possibly help me? Ironically, we both needed the same thing . . . some Divine intervention! Maybe even a miracle.

I was right. It wasn't long before the congregation started asking questions about Father Arnold, his car and his drinking problem. The next thing we knew he was transferred to another church. I understand he did seek help at a treatment center that is specifically aimed at helping clergy with alcohol problems. Apparently they felt that would "solve his problems or at least buy him some more time". I believe he only became more depressed and was left feeling that suicide was the only answer. Shortly thereafter, he committed suicide.

With Father Arnold now dead, I was starting to feel true disappointment and despair. I had gone to the church, been to the doctor, sought out help from my teacher and family . . . but I was getting nowhere. I too was ready to give up and to get it over with.

I began by planning every detail. From how, when and where, right down to the letter I would even leave behind. A letter which I hoped would explain why I had decided to end my life. I decided to end my life at my grandparent's home in Grandma's bedroom. I was supposed to go to work that afternoon but I had said I wasn't feeling well and that I wanted to lay down for a while.

I went into the bathroom first and calmly swallowed a whole bottle of my sleeping pills, one after another until they were all gone. I remember thinking to myself, "I really thought it would somehow be harder than this". But the pills went down so easily. It felt so natural that I took that as a sign it must have been meant to be. Then I calmly looked at myself in the mirror one last time, adjusting my hair, then my make-up. It is almost over. I just need to retrieve the handwritten note that I had written earlier and hidden previously in the clothes shoot of the bathroom. Now to the bedroom. I turned down the short hall towards my grandmother's room, shut the bedroom door behind me and turned the lock. Now for the windows. There were two of them. I checked to ensure that both were locked and pulled the shades all the way down on both of them. I didn't want anyone to be able to look in and see me laying on the bed. All that was left was to lay down and die. I laid down on my Grandmother's bed, placed a blanket over me and set my letter off to one side of me.

I was starting to get tired by now. My eyes grew heavy. The room felt cool and I was glad I had a cover over me. Suddenly I was jolted awake by the sound of someone pounding on the door. It was Grandpa. It must have been time for me to go to work and he was trying to wake me. Then the pounding stopped. I drifted off again deeper and colder. I wished I had another blanket. Then suddenly again, loud banging, this time on the windows. He was trying to get in through the window. Damn it! Couldn't he just leave me alone!

He was going to ruin this for me too! My eyes were getting heavy again. I closed them and drifted off to sleep again. Apparently when they couldn't get through the door they decided to try looking through the window. Since I had it locked and covered there was no chance of that. They now returned to the door, busting through it to get through to me. When they found me unresponsive, they immediately called 911. Grandpa got me up and tried to make me walk, but I couldn't. All I wanted to do was sleep. Again I drifted off to sleep.

My body was limp, I couldn't move, I could hear Grandma's voice in the background saying, "Don't leave me! Come on Bella, Hang On!" *Please* B E L L A!

I heard sirens, and soon the paramedics arrived and began to work on me. Then again I heard Grandma's voice as she said, "Look Bella, this handsome man is going to help you." Great! I thought. Here I am almost dead and once again her priorities are not where they should be. I was soooo sleepy though, very sleepy, and I could care less about her handsome paramedic. My eyes closed again and I fell into a deep sleep.

When I awoke I was in the hospital with doctors and nurses all around me. The lights were so bright, and the doctor was off to one side saying, "Hang on Isabella, you're going to be okay. We need you to throw up. Can you do it on your own? If not we will have to force you to do it. That means pumping your stomach."

"Oh NOOOOOOOOOOOO! I thought. "Can't they just let me die?" The next thing I remember, I was having a tube inserted down my throat. That was all it took, and I started vomiting. To help ease the vomiting, cramps and nausea, they gave me charcoal and some water to sip on. As I became more alert, the doctor questioned me. Did you do this on purpose? Why? I told him it was because of my grandfather, I simply had to get away from him. I just couldn't take it any longer.

The doctor put his head down saying, "Well he wants to see you."

"Tell him **I don't want to see him**", I said, as I rolled over and began to cry. "You should have let me die!"

"Alright, than we're going to have to admit you." he said, "because as long as you feel that way, I can't send you home."

"Good!" I sobbed, "Because I don't want to go back there. EVER!"

The doctor turned to go tell my grandfather that I would be staying. Shortly after that my grandfather appeared by my side.

He looked at me and said, "If you need anything just let me know." Not an, "I'm sorry" or "please forgive me", or "it will never happen again". It was just like nothing had happened all those years. I detested him at that moment.

I ended up spending a total of 5 days in the Psychiatric Unit. It was a locked section of the hospital, the idea was to identify the problem. Once we knew what was going on than we could deal with it, I was told. They told me over and over again how they wanted to help me, and I believed them. However, I was not prepared for what happened during those five days. I was not allowed to have anything like belts, shoelaces, drawstrings, etc. Of course, no sharp items where allowed. I had been knitting a scarf for Christmas and was not allowed to use the knitting needles unless I was, "being supervised". I then had to turn them back into the main desk when I was done.

My time, was which was supposedly my own, wasn't really. There was a fairly strict schedule that I had to adhere to, and I was encouraged to participate in group therapy, art therapy and so on throughout the day. I was checked on every half hour, day and night. I was given medication on a regular basis.

At the end of the five days I made arrangements to go stay with my English teacher from high school. She and I had become good friends and I not only trusted her, but I felt safe with her. I stayed with her until graduation.

After that I moved out of my grandparent's home and into the small apartment owned by my Dad. I was so excited to finally have a place of my own. I really got into decorating it and making it mine. For the first time in my life I was doing really well. I had my own place, a job and decided to go back to college. But this time it was for Criminal Justice classes so I could go into Law Enforcement. There would be no more of me being told what to do and how to do it. I was on my own and I could finally say, things were going right.

Chapter 10

Marriage Annulment

I couldn't wait to turn eighteen. I thought that legally being an adult would magically make everything better for me. I couldn't have been more wrong!

I was now living on my own in my own apartment which I was renting from my Father. He owned a large farm house which years earlier had been remodeled with the upstairs being made into a separate apartment. He also owned the house next door. The plan was to rent out both of them to allow extra income when he retired from the police department. The apartment happened to be empty, and Dad was having some health problems, so I talked him into letting me move in. Not only would it give me some independence, but him some income. I would also be available to take care of him. It sounded like a win-win situation.

However, I was "young and naïve" and literally going from the "frying pan to the fire", as they say. My grandparents had on numerous occasions told me that they, "didn't want me turning out like my mother". In my own mind and heart, I didn't think that was possible. Then I met Todd.

Todd and I met the first week of April 1983. I was preoccupied with school as I was a full time student working on my Associate's Degree. My long term goal was to obtain a Bachelor's Degree in Criminal Justice. I met Todd while taking a Criminal Justice class and my assignment was to interview one of our guest speakers. The instructor had told us that we would get extra credit if we did the additional interviews with one of the guests. Todd was one the first guests to speak. He talked about being a convicted criminal who had committed arson, navigated through the courts, done his time in Joliet Prison and then transformation back into society. As a reformed man he was now working as a carpenter. When class ended I approached him and introduced myself. I explained that we were supposed to interview one of the guest speakers and asked if I could interview him. He answered, "Sure". So we set up a time later in the week to meet at one of the local watering holes.

When I showed up, Todd was already there waiting for me. We quickly went through a series of questions that I had prepared for him. Then the conversation changed to us. He told me that he had been born in Flint and had several brothers that lived locally. His parents also lived in a neighboring city. He had been married before and had a daughter whom he didn't have contact with. He claimed to be a carpenter by trade, working with a small construction group in the Flint area. We seemed to really hit it off, and before the night was over, we had made another date to meet again.

You see, I had picked Todd because I had an interest in prison reform and since that was his topic, it made sense to interview him. We began dating each other the next week. He was thirty-two and I was eighteen. While the age difference didn't bother me, it seemed to bother everybody else. My family and friends all thought he was too old for me. Likewise, I didn't think twice about the fact that I was going to college and he hadn't graduated from high school. Then there was this thing about him having been in prison for arson. I was young, out on my own for only a short time and 'BAM', now I had someone wanting to marry and move in with me. My grandparents were upset with me because I had "disappointed them" by bringing home this old, uneducated man. My dad was upset because I had moved Todd in with me into the apartment above, and my friends all thought I could have done better. Boy, were they ever right! If I would have only listened to everyone concerning this choice.

When I first met Todd, I had had "little dating experience". I was going out with someone on and off from high school for about 4 months, but eventually broke that off because I thought he was getting too serious. Todd, on the other hand, had lots of experience and was living with a woman and her four children. Why did I have trouble seeing the difference between these two? The young man I dated from high school clearly cared about me and treated me well. Todd was totally different, and I just could not see the difference.

We decided to date almost immediately. Our courtship however, wasn't too smooth. We went out a couple of times a week. Usually we'd go to dinner or out walking. I only had a four room apartment. It wasn't really big enough for one, let alone two. When we decided to try living together, he moved in with me instead of looking for a bigger place. Both Todd's parents and mine objected to our dating. Todd's mom felt that there was too much of a social class difference. His dad thought he was too immature. My father and grandparents just flat out didn't like him. They felt he was too old, didn't have a good job, education or the financial means to take care of me. He lost his job, which I'm not sure he really had in the first place. He told me he was a carpenter working with a crew of eight men, but he came and went to work whenever he wanted. When I finally did get a chance to meet one of the guys he was supposedly working with, the man didn't appear to know Todd personally. It was more of having heard of him.

It wasn't long before I ended up losing my job. I had been working in a public library and my boss didn't feel I had worked through my problems yet, as I continued to have a lot of depression surrounding my suicide attempt from six months earlier. While I had been hospitalized for five days, it didn't do any good and I continued to deal with live with my depression on a daily basis.

Another problem was vehicles. I had my own car when I first met Todd. The one he claimed was his turned out to belong to the woman he was living with. He tried to say that he felt sorry for her and gave her the car so that she could have some transportation for her and the kids. Needless to say, he ended up driving my car. "His car" was not really "his car", but his girlfriend's car. This wasn't the first time I caught him lying. The engagement ring he gave me turned out to be stolen from his brother's girlfriend. Once we opened a checking account, and I later found out that he had been writing bad checks. Of course he denied it. On another occasion, he tried to tell me that he was dying of "lung cancer". He had a large scar on his chest that was supposedly from an old injury he received while he working undercover for the Flint Police Department. Then he said, while in prison years later, he was told by the prison doctor that he had a "cancerous growth on one of his lungs". Supposedly he was told that he had "only four years left to live". I was just gullible enough to believe him.

In fact, that was one of the reasons I decided to marry him, even though I never really wanted to get married. I felt sorry for him. He gave me this story about how he was dying and I fell for it. Hook line and sinker!

Another reason was Todd's younger brother's girlfriend. She was sixteen and very pretty. She was bisexual and trying desperately to go straight. Todd's brother came with his own set of problems. He was on drugs, into selling them, drinking, etc. I really felt sorry for his girlfriend, Victoria. She was trying really hard. Even though she was around those kinds of things, she never started using them. She continued to stay in high school for another year and seemed to be doing rather well. We became very close that summer. It was surprising how much alike we were. We both came from the same family backgrounds. But, what nobody knew was that I too was bisexual and that I had begun dating men essentially out of the guilt. Since I was raised Catholic I felt "I had to marry a man". It was bad enough that I didn't want children and had disappointed my grandparents by telling them they would not be having grandchildren.

Both Victoria and I were trying to force ourselves to do what "we thought we should be doing or what society expected of us". I had such a difficult time dealing with my inner most feelings, yet I was honest and shared them with Todd. We had tried to hide our attraction for one another, but eventually the guys found out. This wasn't a problem so much with Todd's brother, but more with Todd. He had always had a fascination with lesbians and a fantasy of doing a Threesome with two women. I found out later that this was more of an obsession than a fantasy. From that day on it was all he talked about. He keep trying to pressure me into setting one up with Victoria. I tried to tell him that either I went straight or I was remained single and gay. I didn't want to be going back and forth as I wanted to be truly committed to one person. He laughed at that and continued to pressure me, sometimes bringing home strange women or expecting me to go out and get them. Soon he began to show signs of jealously, possessiveness and dominance. He was a very jealous, domineering and possessive man. Much like my Grandfather. He also began to lie compulsively and spent our money whether we had it or not. I think I was insecure and lonely before we married, but I'm sure it got worse afterwards.

Our marriage took place on September 2, 1983. It was a civil ceremony performed by Judge Timothy Dawson at Stepping Stones Falls in Flint, Michigan. There were only a handful of people there. I was dressed in a long powered blue dress. Todd wore a brown shirt and slacks. We took no classes beforehand. We met only once prior to the wedding with the Judge. Todd did most of the talking about our future. He spoke of how happy he was going to make me. How he'd take care of me and how I'd never have to work again. But when I brought up how much I wanted to have a career and finish going to school, he'd change the subject.

Those are just some of the things it would have taken to make me happy, however it soon became obvious that we would never be able to have our own home, cars, or much of anything rather quickly because of his compulsive spending. I had always thought marriage should be a partnership comprised of friendship, trust, love and faith. However, I was brought up to believe that this wasn't always the case. My Grandparents wanted us to have our marriage blest, so we made the arrangements and had it done at Holy Redeemer Catholic Church in Burton, Michigan on April 14, 1984. We were involved in marriage preparation classes for almost six weeks. We met with Msgr. Norman Blanchard several times, plus he was also the instructor of our class.

My Grandfather continued to speak ill of Todd until his death on December 14, 1984. At first, I truly believed he loved me and proved it in many ways. However, my reasons were all wrong. First, I had a strong desire to prove to myself that I could go straight and stay that way. Second, I needed to prove to myself and others that I wasn't like my Mother. Third, I had a need to be cared for and loved. I guess I was the only one with doubts for Todd never showed any hesitation. Mine pertained to my feelings toward Victoria. I had a strong premonition that I was making a mistake, but on the other hand, I couldn't justify not marrying to return to a lesbian lifestyle.

The only thing that I felt was unusual at the wedding was the fact that my Victoria, was not allowed to go to it. Both

Todd and his brother would not let her go. This gave me second thoughts.

Our honeymoon was about a year later. We had went up to Tawas, Michigan for the weekend. Once up there, Todd spent all his time looking for other women to bring home "for me". I spent the weekend contemplating suicide. I learned the following Monday that Victoria had overdosed on sleeping pills while I was up north. It was scary, we had become so close that we were like twins. We could actually feel what the other was thinking, feeling or doing even while miles apart. There was one incident that Todd and my Mother-in-law witnessed. After our wedding reception, we gave my Mother-in-law a ride home. Victoria, her boyfriend, Teddy and my Father-in-law were there watching T.V. My Mother-in-law had asked if she could have a couple of flowers from one of the bouquets. While we were picking some out, Victoria came into the room. Up until that point she had not been talking to me. I turned and offered her a blue daisy. She began to cry and said, "I'm sorry you went through with this, but I hope you'll be happy." No one else but Todd and I knew what she meant by this. Todd and I left then and returned home. I suddenly had to agree with her, I too was sorry I had gone through with it. But under the circumstances I was determined to make it work.

At first there wasn't much to adjust to. Todd had always liked to cook. With me having had such a sheltered childhood, I wasn't allowed to do a lot of things around the house like cooking, cleaning and laundering the clothes. So there was a lot he taught me in that respect during the first years. As far as having time together, we had too much time. He would never leave me alone. He was always afraid that I'd go to Victoria and then he'd end up losing me. I would get no privacy at all. If I went to another room he'd be right there wanting to know what I was doing. That even included the bathroom! I felt like I did when I was home with my Grandfather. No privacy whatsoever. I can't say that either of us experienced any homesickness of any sort. But there was certainly lots of times that I wanted to be alone and couldn't. We never had any children. Todd wanted them, and I refused to have any. I had a couple of reasons. First, I didn't want to put a child through the kind of childhood I had had. I'm a firm believer that what happens to you as a child, you will probably do to your children. Second, I didn't want someone like Todd raising our kids. I felt he would abuse them mentally and physically as well as not giving them a good solid moral foundation to build their lives on. And I know I would not have made a good parent.

We started out with excellent communication. However, he used it against me. I was very honest and open about everything. But this only caused more problems. And he would only be as honest as he wanted to be. For example, I was honest about my feelings for Victoria. He took that knowledge and used it to get what he wanted and all the while saying he was doing it for me. I was so depressed that he talked Victoria into coming over and being friends. I guess he thought seeing her would cheer me up. When she did come over it was to tell me how her boyfriend had been beating her up and slipping drugs into her food in an effort to get her to sleep with him. She had dropped out of school and become just as depressed as I was. On top of that, her Mother had kicked her out leaving her with no home and she didn't want to stay with her boyfriend anymore. Her Mother was, like mine, driven by two other priorities, money and men. Todd suggested that she move in with us. It was a nice gesture, however, I didn't want him to be around her and he knew it. But he was only interested in getting his fantasy fulfilled. Victoria being there put me in the middle and under considerable pressure. They were both using it to their advantage.

Victoria was trying one last time to make me give up the idea of going straight and making the marriage work. And Todd was going to prove that he could have his cake and eat it too. This went on for almost 3 months. I came close to having a nervous breakdown, started drinking, lost sleep and 23 pounds. I almost ended up in the hospital. It ended when she called me at one day to say she was leaving. She wouldn't give me an explanation either. I came home to find her crying and packing. She left and I didn't hear from her until almost two months later. She called me from the hospital to tell me that she had just had a miscarriage. When I got there she explained that Todd had raped her the day she left. Again, I felt to blame. It was my love for her that had put her in her in this awful position. Would she ever be able to forgive me? I couldn't blame her if she didn't. I returned home with the realization that my honesty and feelings for Victoria had been a big problem in our marriage.

Todd was so excessively jealous and possessive. He would follow me wherever I went. I found out one spring while doing my spring cleaning that he had even had the house bugged and installed a two-way mirror in one room. If I had to leave to go somewhere he'd follow me or keep phoning me to make sure I was where I said I'd be. I had to give up all my friends because of him. The male friends would get tired of his attitude and the way he treated them. The female friends got tired of him trying to get them to sleep with him. It was hard after that to even make any friends. Male or female. I got to the point where I didn't even try anymore. I didn't go outside at all. I got tired of being accused of sleeping with everyone so I spent all my time inside like a prisoner. He would be gone for hours at a time with no explanation. Yet if I were so much as a few minutes late we would end up arguing for hours or days. It got to the point where we argued about everything. He couldn't save money, yet he refused to let me budget it. Our bills were paid late if he paid them at all so naturally that caused more fighting.

I tried dealing with these problems as best I could with what I had, but it didn't make much of a difference. I don't know if Todd ever cheated on me with anyone that I didn't know about during the first couple of years. I had my doubts about the last two years, however. I later found out through Todd that he was picking up woman and telling them that I was his daughter. My nerves got so bad that the doctor finally put me on tranquilizers. They helped for a while, but they weren't getting to the root of the problem. I was afraid of him and myself. There were four or five times that Todd became physically abusive. Each time it started with an argument, then when I didn't want to fight anymore I'd get up and try to leave. He wouldn't let me go. He'd tie me up, hold me down, lock me in a room or take the phone away. I was lucky enough not to get hurt badly. I usually ended up with some cuts, bruises and sore muscles, but nothing worse than that.

We also had constant inference from both families. My family would continually tell us that we should be doing better than we were. His family kept dragging him down instead of encouraging him. We had to rely a lot on my family because his family had no money. Todd was constantly asking me to borrow money from my Dad. My Dad didn't mind helping me out, but he didn't like Todd using it for things we didn't need. We had to rent the apartment from my Dad because we couldn't afford anything else. Besides that Todd wasn't responsible enough to see that the rent was paid on time. We wouldn't have been able to get away with paying it late all the time somewhere else.

Throughout our marriage I continued to suffer with severe depression and had to seek treatment several times.

The night I decided to get the divorce, was based on one event that was like the straw that broke the camel's back. I had come home to find Todd getting ready to go to the college to give a lecture. The class would be over at 7:00pm, so he'd be home by 7:20 he said. I laid down to get some sleep before going into my second job which started at midnight. I woke up at 10:30 and he still wasn't home. As I was getting ready I realized that the phone bill and a card I had bought for my Mother's birthday hadn't been mailed yet. I started to leave about ten minutes early so that I could stop to get stamps and gas. As I was getting into my car, Todd pulled into the driveway. He didn't bother saying hello, but instead demanded to know where I was going so early. He never attempted to explain where he had been for the last three hours. I was so mad and angry that I told him that if he didn't have to tell me where he had been, then it wasn't any of his business where I was going.

I told Todd the next day that I wanted a divorce. I explained to him that I didn't love him and it was stupid to keep telling myself that I could learn to. I was only learning to hate the sight and sound of him. His jealous and possessiveness along with his following and checking up on me was more than I could tolerate. I was tired of putting my life on hold. I was becoming someone I hated. He was slowly draining the life from me. I actually felt the decision to get a divorce was my idea. We had discussed it several other times, but I just never seemed to be able to go through with it. I guess I was just too stubborn and proud to admit that it wasn't working out.

I went to see a friend of mine on June 3, 1987. Patrick was the only friend that I still had. He had helped me through the past two years with his friendship and encouragement. He was the only person that I felt I could trust and talk to. He never did like Todd, but I think he understood to some degree why I couldn't leave him. It was Patrick who got me to stop drinking and in to see a psychologist named Kevin. He also prevented me from committing suicide once and leaving the state another time. When I met with Patrick, I was really upset. He sat me down and tried to get me to talk about what was going on, but I just couldn't. All I wanted to do was run away, but I knew Todd would find me and punish me for it. Patrick wanted me to go talk to Kevin, but I told him that Kevin had refused to see me again unless I either filed for or got a divorce. Patrick made it clear that he would still support my decision no matter what, but he felt that my life was in danger and that I should make a decision soon. He was right, I couldn't put it off any longer. I had already threatened to kill Todd or myself if our situation did not change, so I agreed to let Patrick make an appointment for me the next day.

Kevin wanted to hospitalize me immediately. But I wanted to do this on my own. I filed for the divorce on June 4th. Todd moved out in mid-July. He wouldn't go any sooner because he didn't think I was serious and still said that he had nowhere else to go. Then when he finally did agree to move out, he took his time. He told a friend of mine that he really didn't promise to change, but he did say that he didn't want the divorce.

We had earlier sought counseling on several occasions. There was no opposition to going, but Todd never tried to correct his problems because he never felt that he had any. The problems he felt were always mine. The first time, we went to a child psychiatrist because we both felt that most of my problems stemmed from my childhood. She agreed to some point, but said a lot of the problems came from a chemical imbalance. She treated me for that, but it didn't help. She also tried to treat Todd, but he refused to admit that he had a problem or even try.

The second attempt was with a well-known marriage counselor. He came right out and told us that "we didn't have an ice-cubes chance in hell if we stayed together". Those were his words. He refused to treat us after that stating that it wouldn't do any good and that it would be in our best interest to seek a divorce. Then if after that one or both wanted to come back he'd be more than happy to help.

I made a third attempt to find out if what had happened during my childhood could have caused all these problems. I had been diagnosed with Dissociative Amnesia as I had a number of years as a child and young teen that I could not remember anything about.

I had memories that been unconsciously blocked due to the memory being associated with a high levels of stress or trauma. This type of amnesia is not unusual for people who have suffered traumatic or stressful situations. I basically had blocked out about twelve years of my childhood. We determined that I had been sexually and physically abused. Then with the break-up of my parents, my Mother's rejection, all of this adding to my depression. Then when Todd came along it got worse.

The fourth attempt was with a psychologist who worked with a psychiatrist. They wanted Todd to come in for treatment, but he refused. They felt that there wasn't much they could work on as long as Todd and I remained married. So they suggested a separation or divorce. I was still too stubborn to do that so I gave up.

Up to that point I had always been the one to suggest getting help. But one day Todd told me that there was a new program at work that he was willing to try. I didn't believe it would do any good so I wouldn't go. If after all these years the professionals kept telling us to get a divorce then they must have seen something that we hadn't. After all, they were in the business of making money, it didn't make sense to turn us away if there wasn't a good reason.

Todd tried to get me to give him another chance, but I wouldn't. He tried to say that in the past it was always one or the other trying to make things work instead of both trying together. He was right. I think by this point though, he wanted the divorce just as badly as I did, but was afraid to be the one to file for it. Once he was out of the house I didn't want him to come back. I started doing better in school and at work. His being gone made a big improvement on my life and outlook on things. I even started going to church again. No one in the family encouraged any type of reconciliation. My family during the previous separations had encouraged me to get a divorce, but they didn't do anything this time. I don't think they thought I was serious about it this time either.

During our separation Todd constantly called and followed me around. He would stop at work and bother me. And he always started out the same way. He'd want to know where I'd been, who I was it. At one point I had an incident where "someone" tried to blow up my car. At first he admitted to it, then when the police showed up he denied it. They never were able to prove anything, but he had done time for arson before we were married. He continued to harass me by driving by house on his way to his new girlfriends who lived only a few streets behind me. He then moved in with another woman a couple of weeks after that. I, on the other hand, stayed by myself with my four cats of which I eventually granted custody.

When I filed for my civil divorce, my attorney asked me to provide him with a copy of our marriage license. After searching through the house and not being able to locate our copy, I went to the court house to get another one.

What happened next, left me speechless and in shock.

The clerk asked for both our names so as to locate our license. I was not prepared for her next question. "Which one do you want copies of?"

Thinking she clearly must have made a mistake, I said, "There should be only one with our names, but my husband was married once before."

She then asked me for his date of birth. After I gave it to her she got a puzzle look on her face and said, "Can you recognize his signature if I show it to you?"

"Yes, of course", I said.

She disappeared to the file cabinets and shortly returned with several documents in her hand.

The clerk said, "Please check these and tell me which one is your husband's signature?", as she laid them down on the counter in front of me.

I slowly looked at each document. My heart was now starting to beat faster. "How could this be?" I said. "He told me he was only married once?"

"I think we have a problem here" she said. "What is the name of your attorney? I think we need to call him."

By now I was dazed, the tears were rolling down my face as I began shaking uncontrollably. Todd had lied to me all these years. There had not been one wife as he had said, but in fact four and maybe even a fifth one out of state.

The clerk tried to comfort me.

"You stay here honey and sit down. I'm going to go call your attorney and we're going to figure out what you need to do next."

As I sat there thinking back to the beginning of my marriage, it was now clear that I was married to a pathological liar. He had lied about so many things. His life, his job, his car, my engagement ring, everything. I buried my head in my hands and began to sob.

After a short time, the clerk returned and said, "I talked to your attorney. Your husband lied on your marriage license. This is considered fraud. I'm going to give you copies of his previous marriage licenses to give to your attorney. You're to contact him and he'll help you get through this. Everything is going to be okay."

I couldn't wait to get home to examine the contents of the envelope the clerk had given me. Once home, I opened it and pulled out the copies of each marriage license. I couldn't help but think, "Did these women go through the same thing I had?" I called my attorney and made an appointment for the next day.

The following day I drove downtown to meet with him. He told me that my marriage was over except for the legalities. All that I had to do now was make it through my day in court. He also told me, based on what he knew about my husband, he probably would not show up to contest it and that it should go smoothly. I keep telling myself that it would be over soon. Just stay strong. Easier said than done.

My Divorce was granted on August 24, 1987 based on fraud. Todd had told me of only one marriage prior to ours and since he didn't divorce her that was the grounds for our divorce. He never showed up to contest our divorce. He also owed $1,550 at that time in child support which he was refusing to pay. Hardly a surprise right?

I also went on to file for an Annulment through the Catholic Church. It was granted on December 28, 1987. I had been Catholic since the age of seven when I was baptized. Todd also said he was Catholic, however, we were never able to find paperwork to prove that he had been baptized. When applying for an Annulment within the Catholic Church, you must prove certain things before they will grant it. Usually it only takes one thing, but in our case I had documentation of so many that it was "cut and dry" as they say.

Following is a list of the grounds the Church used to annul my marriage to Todd. Each is listed by name, code number and a brief description of the code.

Psychic-natured incapacity to assume marital obligations (Canon 1095, 30) you or your spouse, at the time of consent, was unable to fulfill the obligations of marriage because of a serious psychological disorder or other condition.

Error about a quality of a person (Canon 1097, sec. 2)
You or your spouse intended to marry someone who either possessed or did not possess a certain quality, e.g., social status, marital status, education, religious

conviction, freedom from disease, or arrest record. That quality must have been directly and principally intended.

Fraud (Canon 1098) Reasons for Marriage Annulment

You or your spouse was intentionally deceived about the presence or absence of a quality in the other. The reason for this deception was to obtain consent to marriage

Willful exclusion of children (Canon 1101, sec. 2)

You or your spouse married intending, either explicitly or implicitly, to deny the other's right to sexual acts open to procreation.

Willful exclusion of marital fidelity (Canon 1101, 12)

You or your spouse married intending, either explicitly or implicitly, not to remain faithful

Lack of new consent during convalidation (Canons 1157, 1160)

After your civil marriage, you and your spouse participated in a Catholic ceremony and you or your spouse believed that (1)

you were already married, (2) the Catholic ceremony was merely a blessing, and (3) the consent given during the Catholic ceremony had no real effect. [R7]

I then went to court to get a civil Annulment which was filed for and granted in May of 1994. To obtain this civil annulment you again have to prove that the marriage was null and void. In our case Todd had been previously married and that marriage had not been legally terminated prior to us marrying.

During our divorce and annulment processes I did my best to be "civil" with Todd whenever I saw him. I gave up a lot of myself during those years to try and make him happy. And in return I lost a lot of myself. The truth was I hated him and was very angry at him. I had a hard time forgiving him for using me and taking advantage of me. Yes, I was dumb, young and naïve, but that shouldn't make it open season for "use and abuse". That being said, I have tried very hard to recover from most everything that happened to me during those years.

Todd went on to remarry, divorce and remarry over and over again until his death on July 09, 2010. From what records I can find and what his family has said it looks like he has been married around ten times. Move over Elizabeth Taylor! You've got some completion.

Chapter 11

A Man with a Gun

After all the problems both emotionally and physically concerning my marriage and divorce/annulment, I was ready to start a new life. It was somewhat "refreshing" to go upstairs to my small apartment. I knew that Todd would not be there. I was starting to feel safe again after many years of always having to look over my shoulder.

There was one weekday that I stopped by to help my dad with his bills. I walked up the steps to the landing and knocked on the closed door which lead to his kitchen. From the other side, I heard his voice, but there was something different in the tone. It sounded distant and confused in a way I had never heard before. As I quickly listened again, there was a very distinct sound of a gun cocking on the other side of the door. I felt chills running down my body, and the hairs on the back of my neck were now standing straight up. "Did I actually hear what I thought I just heard?" I thought to myself, as I instinctively took a step to my right and flattened myself against the wall as much as I could. That sound of a gun cocking, is a hard one to mistake. I tried to compose myself and said, "Dad, are you okay? It's Bella. I'm here to help you with the bills". I tried to rationalize why he would be acting this way. Maybe it was the alcohol, or had he finally gone off the deep end?—I truly didn't know.

But if all this wasn't enough, he then retorted, "Who are you? What do you want?"

This question now shook me to the core, and I again said, "Dad, it's me, Bella, your daughter. I've come to help you with the bills."

There was a long silence, then he said, "I don't have a daughter. Go away. I don't know who you are. If you don't go away, I'll shoot you." I stood still for a moment, only my eyes blinking as those words echoed in my head. Was he serious? How could he say such a thing? I was his flesh and blood who had been taking care of him for years now. What had happened to make him say such a thing? Did he really not know who I was? Then suddenly warm tears started to roll down my checks I was jolted back into existence by him saying once again that he would shoot me if I didn't leave.

Now I had to think like a cop. I knew he had guns and that he knew how to use them, and even though he was my father, I had to assume he would use them because he said he would. It was time to act. I slid along the wall, down the landing as quietly as I could, then out the door and up the stairs to my apartment where I called 911. This was not a good situation. Dad was a trained marksman who had half a dozen weapons in the house. He was acting erratic and we had to do something immediately or someone would get hurt. I asked for a good friend of mine who I worked with on the police department. I explained to him that my father, who was once a Police Officer, was now barricaded in his home with guns and threating to use them on me. We needed to act quickly.

Within minutes two officers arrived and met with me. Once there one asked if I had tried again to make contact with him. "Are you kidding?" I said, "He's already threatened to kill me twice." Then another officer turned to me a said, "Yes, but he's less likely to actually take a shot at you than he is at one of us. So please, let's make one more attempt, ok?" Well, he did have a point, but I wasn't thrilled with the idea of walking back up those steps again where I would be in the line of fire, instead I decided to stand at the base of steps where I could yell up to up to Dad.

As one officer held the screen door open, I stood just inside the doorway at the bottom of the steps and said, "Dad, It's me, Bella. Could you put the gun down and come outside for a minute. There's a couple of friends of yours from the department here that want to talk to you. They came to visit you." I stopped to listen for a response. There was nothing, but silence.

Then one of the officers grabbed my arm and pulled me outside the landing.

"You know what this means, right?"

"Yes, just let me try one more time, please."

They looked at other. By this time I had tears in my eyes. "Please, I beg of you, he's one of us."

"Okay, one more time, but that's it. If you can't get him to come out, this will be considered a barricaded gunman situation. He will no longer be one of us."

As I stepped back inside the landing, I took a deep breath and tried to sound as calm as I could be. It was time for a different approach.

"Mr. Zimmerman", I said, "I understand that you were a police officer. Is that true?"

After a short pause I heard, "Yes, a detective,"

"Wow, that's really impressive. I've always wanted to be a detective", I answered. I felt I was finally making some progress.

"Could I come in and talk to you? Maybe see some of your guns", I asked? With that, I could hear noise coming from behind the door. Dad was removing the barricade. The officers and I made eye contact. "Yes! We're in!" Finally some progress. I remember walking up the four steps, counting each one out loud in my mind and thinking, "Am I going to make it to the top? Is he still holding a gun on the door? Is he going to shoot me? Is this how it's going to end for me?"

One step, two steps, three steps, four, and then finally the top one. I paused on that one and reached for the door knob. It seemed like a million miles away. I remember thinking to myself that I should have put a vest on. Too late now. I was visibly shaking, inside and out, as I reached for the door knob. I must try to calm myself. With that, I opened the door and quickly stepped to the side. There he sat at the far side of the grey kitchen table with an S&W Chief's special handgun lying next to his hand. It was his back-up revolver while he was on the department.

The two officers were not far behind and were waiting for a signal from me. As I walked into the kitchen, I saw that he was slouched in his chair with his underwear hanging down around his feet. I was so embarrassed and humiliated. This was the first time I had ever seen my grown father naked. For a moment I wasn't sure what to do. Should I grab the gun or his underwear first? I had hoped one of the male officers would step in and help him. Finally, when I assessed he was no longer a threat, I walked up to him and gently pulled his underwear up to where it belonged. Funny how I was more concerned about his dignity at that point than getting the gun away from him. Although I do remember seeing one of the officers out of the corner of my eye taking it in while I was pulling up Dad's underwear.

I knew Dad was an alcoholic. What I just didn't realize was how long he had been drinking and what the long term effects of the alcohol had done to his body.

He was in bad physical and mental shape and I didn't truly understand it until that day when I saw him naked in the kitchen. It was then that I realized how very sick he really was. My father was what many call a "functioning or secret alcoholic". While there were many "warning signs" to those around him, many chose to ignore them. He drank on a daily basis, often alone, before or after going out. He would sip all day and night from a bottle that was a mixture of whiskey and coca cola. Hiding bottles in the kitchen cabinets behind other cans, jars and boxes, and in the bathroom cabinets. As well as in the living room stashed under furniture and cushions. While whiskey was his preferred drink, he would often mix it with coca cola, so that to others it looked like he was drinking only coca cola. He was constantly late or would not show up for family events saying he didn't feel well. Granted his health was declining due to the alcohol, but again he blamed it on his back or his stomach or nerves.

Since he had his parents raising me, Sundays were suppose our day together. He would pick me up from Grandma's house and we would go to see a movie followed by dinner. He was always late though. I would often find myself staring out the window, wondering where he was and why he was late. I so looked forward to our times together even if they weren't the best. I just wanted to get out of the house and be with my Father who I idolized. During the week he would often be late. After he retired from the police department he worked as a Barber at Larry's Barber Shop. When his lateness became a problem, my grandfather, who was also a barber would go and cover for him until he could make it in, which was usually midmorning or sometimes closer to noon. Dad kept saying that his back was the problem. Then we noticed his hands as they would tremble uncontrollably making it hard for him to cut hair. He then became withdrawn, depressed, moody, and eventually lost interest in the things that he once loved. Here again those around him "covered for him" making excuses when we should have been getting help for him.

Suddenly I was brought back to the present by one of the officers elbowing me and saying, "Mr. Zimmerman, I think you should go to the hospital and get checked out."

My dad just stared off into space, not saying or doing anything.

It was then I decided it was up to me and said, "Dad, these nice men have called an ambulance for you so you don't have to worry about driving."

But he said, "I'm not sick." as the ambulance attendants came up the steps.

"But you don't look so good Dad. Let's just go to the hospital and let them check you out, ok?"

Obviously this approach wasn't working; time for another. He was also a diabetic, so I decided to give that one a try.

"You know Dad, you've been having problems with your sugar. They could check it out while you're there?"

He seemed to be thinking about it. "How about I get your brother to take you? Would you like that?" I asked. I can give Uncle Jim a call?

Dad perked up a little when I mentioned his brother's name, but I didn't want to leave him to go into the other room where the phone was. I turned to one of the officers and asked him to go call Dad's, brother, Jim who was at work at General Motors and my sister, Diane.

What happened next told just how bad off Dad really was. He reached into his pockets and started pulling out pieces of lint, after which he would make motions in the air as if he were counting them. When I asked what he was doing, he replied, "I'm counting my money. I don't want anyone to take my money." With tears in my eyes, I asked him to please pick up his money and put it back in his pocket where it would be safe. With the help of one of the two officers I got Dad dressed. By that time, he finally agreed to go to the hospital, but he would not go by ambulance. His brother Jim arrived shortly thereafter and took him by car to the emergency room of Hurley Hospital.

Diane and I stayed behind on the advice of the police officers. We knew he had more than one gun. So our objective was to search through the house and find not only the guns, but all of his remaining liquor bottles. "Search through the house and find them all before he comes home," the officers said. "He probably has places he secretly hides his liquor". Well, he did. We found bottles in the oven, the kitchen cabinets, the fridge, and the bathroom, his desk, under furniture cushions and behind furniture. We also found a number of weapons.

What we didn't know then was that he would not be coming home. He was admitted straight from the emergency room and later that night, went into a coma. He stayed in that coma for just under two weeks until he died. During that time I was working on my Bachelor's Degree and would often stop on my way home from school to visit him. I found it particularly hard to watch him deteriorate and wondered if there was anything I, or anyone else, could have done that might have made a difference.

For the longest time I was so angry at my grandmother and the others for not believing that he was an alcoholic.

Every day that I took Grandma to visit Dad, she would stand over him shaking her head and hands saying, "I didn't know. Damn it, if I would have just known I could have done something!" Right about then I wanted to wring her neck. And that was putting it nicely! I KNEW and I had told her over and over again. There was no reason on earth that would account for why she "didn't know". She simply choose to deny it. After all she was used to making excuses and denying things. That same denial was what allowed me to be sexually and mentally abused for years right in front of her without her choosing to do anything.

In retrospect, Dad began drinking as a young man. His first wife Connie was an alcoholic. His second wife, Maggie, a barmaid, also drank regularly and heavily, as she was bartender and managed many bars over the years for a living. In addition, with Dad being a Police Officer, he saw a lot of violence, distress and death. The anxiety of such a profession often leads to alcohol abuse. In the end, it caused problems with his marriages, his career, his family, his health and ultimately lead to his death. Knowing now what type of childhood he had and how he was raised, he must have felt like such a failure alone and ashamed. What an awful way to die.

Chapter 12

Sticks and Stones

Me in Uniform

Sticks and stones
will break my bones
but names will ne~~v~~er hurt me.

We've all heard this nursery rhyme, but how many of us
have actually thought about what it meant? I chose to use

it because it as illustrates so well how damaging something like gossip can be.

Gossip it can cause serious irreversible damage; relationships can be destroyed, families torn apart, jobs affected, and so on. I am here to tell you that gossip can, and did, destroy my family, my relationships, my friendships, my career, and *MY LIFE* up to this point. You may ask, "How can a few words do that?" Well, when I was growing up, as you may remember, my dream always was to go into law enforcement. With Dad having been a police officer, I think it was sort of in my blood, so to speak. I worked long and hard at three jobs to obtain a Bachelor's Degree in Criminal Justice. I started out my career doing plain clothes, undercover work. Then after a few years, I switched to the patrol division. It was during this time that I helped launch the COP Program which stands for Community Oriented Policing program. While I did have a patrol vehicle, I spent a great deal of time on foot walking and getting to know the people within my assigned area. Since we were known as a "service oriented department" we did a number of vehicle jump-starts, unlocks, building checks, alarm verifications, etc. All of this helped to build a proactive partnership between the police and the citizens that helped to identify and solve problems before they happened. I also worked to became certified as an Apprentice Counselor and as a Paralegal during this time period.

After that I spent a few years working in dispatch. I can honestly say I didn't enjoy that as much as being out on the street, but that position is the probably the most essential and demanding of all the jobs I had within the department. Some of the officers looked at the dispatcher job as though they were "non-essential or cushy". I think it was just the opposite. As a dispatcher you were responsible for maintaining communications between the headquarters, officers in the field, outside emergency and law enforcement agencies and the public. You had to take and screen calls, enter them into the computer, dispatch the information to the officer and then if the officer wanted any warrant or record checks, you had to run those. All of which while you are handling walk-ins, other calls from phone and radio. It definitely required the ability to think clearly, quickly and multitask.

I mention this because during this time I continued to get excellent job evaluations, even though I was still struggling with my depression. Throughout this time period, I sought treatment outside of work with a Psychiatrist. In addition to my depression, I still had years of childhood memories that I had blocked out. My Psychiatrist believed it was a form of amnesia that was due to the abuse I went through as a child. It possibly was something I might have seen that was related to the kidnapping and murder of Robert Boileau. Again, all of this was done outside of work. I never told any of my fellow employees or anyone else about this; I kept it a secret! At one point I found a Psychiatrist in Cincinnati, Ohio who did Sodium Pentothal Interviews. After careful research and thought I decided to go to Cincinnati and undergo one of these interviews with the hope that I might retrieve some of my lost memories. I took with me a friend who worked with the FBI. He had a special interest in the trip since some of the memories I hoped to retrieve would aid the FBI in solving the yet unsolved kidnapping and murder cold case of Robert Boileau from November 1969. (He also had read the FBI's report's on this case. This is important as both of us saw those reports and know they existed at one time. Later when I went to request a copy of them – they had mysteriously disappeared!) While I was obviously anxious, I was also hopeful that I might finally get some of my memories back after all these years. How cool would that be!

We arrived in Cincinnati and meet with the doctor at his office. We talked about how the procedure was to be done, how long it would take, where it would be done, what to expect afterwards and so on. It was to be done the following day at the nearby Jewish hospital as an outpatient procedure. There would be the doctor, an anesthesiologist and a couple of nurses to assist them. The procedure itself was fairly simple. I tried to not get my hopes up, but I would be lying if I said I wasn't expecting a small miracle.

The next day seemed to take forever to arrive. I was really nervous as I laid on the table waiting for the doctor to administer the Sodium Pentothal. I had so many questions racing through my mind. Would I remember anything with regards to the case? Was it possible that we could bring some closure to this case after all these years? Would I remember more incidents of abuse?

It was then the doctor's voice broke in and said, "Isabella, you have to calm down. Your blood pressure is going up and your heart is racing. Take a couple of deep breathes and focus. Let me know when you are you ready?"

I slowly inhaled trying to concentrate on my breathing and not on what was about to happen.

"Ok", I said, "I'm ready."

"Fine, let's get started then," he said, as he turned on the cassette recorder and laid it on my chest. He turned to the IV and began to inject the Sodium Pentothal. I started to feel sleepy and I remember from our previous conversation that "you had to have just the right amount of Sodium Pentothal or the person would fall asleep". It was then that I heard his voice as he started asking me a series of prepared questions concerning my childhood and the time that was "missing". I wanted to know more about the abuse. I had a fairly large chunk of time missing. Clearly something or someone had caused me to block it out. The question was could we retrieve it? Then we were interested in the crime. Did I know anything about it that might help solve it if it were reopened? The next thing I remember was the doctor shaking me and saying, "It's ok Isabella, open your eyes you're safe". Just like that it was over. I had been crying and I was cold. I thought I'd be more awake and alert, but not so. I tended to be so sleepy I was slurring and having a hard time answering their questions. They gave me a warm blanket as I asked, did it work? "I think you got some of the answers you were looking for", the doctor said, "But we'll talk later, ok?" The nurses unhooked me and asked me to sit there for a few minutes to make sure I was ok before trying to get dressed. My friend and I went to lunch across the street from the hospital to a Hungarian Restaurant. We were excited to try it since I was Hungarian. Later that afternoon we met the doctor at his office to discuss what had happened.

"Well", the doctor said, "There's no doubt in my mind that you were sexually abused by your grandfather and possible someone else". It alone could account for the amnesia you have. He went to tell me it's called Psychological or Dissociative Amnesia. He then discussed the rest of the results with us before we returned home. While I didn't get a play by play that filled in all the blanks for me, I did get enough memories that helped me to fill in some of the larger gaps, making the smaller ones easier to deal with. (That was the only time I saw that doctor) I came home and continued seeing a therapist on the side.

Then in early 1995, I began experiencing severe lower abdominal pain. I contacted my primary care doctor and set up an appointment to see her. She immediately wanted me to undergo tests to rule out cancer since it strongly ran in my family. I was naturally troubled and worried as four of my five aunts died of cancer. Not thinking anything of it, I confided in a co-worker as to why I was taking time off work when she asked. Shortly after that, I was called into my supervisor's office when I arrived for work one day. I was then told that there were "rumors circulating about me and that I was to go home until we could get them straightened out". Laughing out loud I said, "Rumors? What kind of rumors? You're joking right?" "No", he said, "I'm sorry Isabella, but this is serious." I again asked him, "Ok, what rumors? It appears that there are rumors circulating that you are dying of terminal cancer, that you have a case of ringworm you are intentionally using it to infect other persons with and finally, that you have been impregnated by an alien from outer space."

At this point I didn't know whether to laugh or cry. This was too much. How could you think such a thing let alone have the nerve to say it? Here I was waiting for test results to come back to find out if I had uterine or ovarian cancer and my coworkers were making a joke about it. I didn't understand why anyone would think that would be funny. I certainly didn't think it was. I did actually have a case of ringworm on my leg. I don't to this day know where I got it from. It was a real and costly problem for me as I had two cats at the time and I had to not only get treated myself, but I also had to have them treated. I didn't realize at first that ringworm could be passed back and forth between animal and human and then back to animal again if not properly treated. So my initial treatment didn't work until I realized that we were merely passing it back and forth, and that we all had to be treated at one time. I can honestly say that I wasn't lying. I was not trying to intentionally infect others that I worked with. I got treatment immediately and did everything I was supposed to, and I could prove it with all the necessary paperwork.

As far as the third rumor goes, I could honestly say, I have NEVER had sex with an alien. HA! Even if such a thing were possible, even if there were aliens; no way, no how, period! Ha Again!

Regardless of that explanation, I was sent home that afternoon and told not to return until we could straighten this out. The next day I went to my doctor and got what medical paperwork I needed to return, however when I turned it in, I was still told that I could not return to work and was never given a reason. This went on for three months until I was forced to consume all of my accrued sick time and was placed on indefinite medical leave. I decided it was time to obtain an attorney. I was mad. DAMN MAD! I had worked for the police department for long time. This was my career and I had received excellent evaluations up to this point, and now these rumors regarding me began to circulate throughout the department. This all cost me time, money and caused me untold emotional distress not to mention that they seriously defamed me. Even more serious at this point, however, was my "status" with the department. I was ordered to undergo both a psychological and a psychiatric examination. Since the department did not allow me to view these reports, I had to have my attorney fight to get them. It got to the point that I had no choice. My career, my retirement, my reputation, my name, everything that I had worked so hard for was at stake. The department wanted to say "I was unfit for duty" and I simply could not let that happen. I went to both examinations and a third evaluation that was conducted by a doctor of our choosing.

The department sent me to two doctors. At one I underwent a psychological evaluation, and at the other, I underwent a psychiatric evaluation. It was the opinion of the first doctor that I had a delusional disorder and should be treated with medication. That also led to the conclusion that I was, "not fit for duty as an officer". The second doctor's evaluation relied heavily on my previous history of depression, and although I denied making any bizarre statements, she wrote that they and the behaviors were evidence of dissociative episodes. Likewise, she used my admission of poor memory as evidence of dissociative episodes. She too concluded that I psychologically, was not fit to perform my job functions. We then decided that I would go to a doctor of my choice for an unbiased opinion. This doctor saw me on two occasions. The first visit was taken up with a mountainous pile of documents that I had collected over my lifetime, in my search of information about my family and childhood. I suffered from Dissociative Amnesia and had a number of years "missing" from my childhood which I believed was due to the abuse I went through. My search to recover those memories has become an obsession at times. As previously noted in November of 1994, I went to Cincinnati, Ohio to have a Sodium Pentothal interview done to try and retrieve whatever memories I could. I also recall trying hypnosis as well as other types of therapies.

On the second appointment, I had a more formal mental status examination done and was <u>not</u> found to be unfit for duty. This doctor took into account that I had a psychiatric past of depression, but that it was not relevant since I had worked satisfactorily for a long time. In his opinion, my obsessiveness and compulsiveness had not spilled over into my employment. His report ended by saying that I should not be forced to seek treatment or take medication by my employer for illnesses or symptoms I did not have. So it was now "us" against them. I hadn't worked in months, was forced to use all my sick and vacation time, and there was no sign that they were going to allow me to return to work. My law enforcement career of nearly fifteen years was on the line. When everything was said and done would it all go down the drain?

So now I have been "labeled" as "mentally ill" (Bi-polar to be exact). I eventually got my job back, but that meant taking them to court. And that "label or stigmatism" forced me to take an early retirement which ended my career in law enforcement. After all, what police department is going to hire a mentally ill person and allow them to carry a gun?

I still feel the pain and anger of those days and months. I never did find out who started those rumors and it doesn't matter at this point, although I feel someone should have been held accountable. Is it right to ruin someone's life and career like that? The hell I went through during those nine months was preposterous. What depression I was suffering with beforehand, was nothing in comparison to what I dealt with during this ordeal. As it is often said, "I wouldn't wish it on my worst enemy!"

Chapter 13

Survivors

With my law enforcement career behind me, I thought that there must be something in the private sector I could do that would allow me to use my education and experience. I put out some feelers and was fortunate enough to find a position as an On-Call Coordinator with a nonprofit organization that offered comprehensive services for survivors of domestic violence, sexual assault and child abuse. Another reason I felt so comfortable working there, was that we not only had lesbians on our staff, but it worked at addressing same-sex domestic violence and sexual assaults. Something we did not adeptly address on the police department.

I began working as their On-Call Coordinator in March of 1999. It was a job I feel I was well suited for and truly felt I was good at it. I enjoyed empowering clients through education and support. I personally supervised, trained and coordinated the On-Call Response Team which was comprised of 23 on-call volunteers and paid staff. My teams responded to scenes of domestic violence, sexual assault, and child abuse throughout the county providing crisis intervention, counseling, legal advocacy, shelter, information, referrals, and more. I was very proud of my team.

When I first began working there though, their reputation with the area police departments was not that good. I worked hard at rebuilding the trust and respect that had been missing between them and the seven police departments throughout the county. I created a new response protocol for the police to use when responding to domestic and sexual assault calls. I met with each of the seven police departments, taking time to not only introduce myself, but to answer their questions and concerns about the new protocol. My attempt was to alleviate any past animosities and illicit their assistance in creating the new countywide protocol. This of course, all took time, because they were not only leery of me, but our organization. The officers had a lot of valid concerns about my team, such as why in the past there was no response, late response, refusal to respond to a scene when no arrest had been made, (even if the scene was secure), the giving of erroneous information about working with a male victims and arguing with an officer about how to do his job or even questioning why an arrest wasn't made and poor attitudes. These were just some of the complaints I encountered. I realized when I was first hired, that the poor working relationship with the police had to be corrected before I could make the program work. I created a laminated police protocol card with the protocol on one side and our services on the reverse side. This card was then distributed to all the county police agencies. I then updated and distributed new business cards, informational brochures and handouts to the police departments, hospital, court and social service agencies.

Another major part of my job involved working with the volunteers. I was not only responsible for their training, but for establishing a master contact list, planning schedules, new more convenient paperwork, the setting up of safety courses, facilitating self-defense classes, instructing debriefing sessions and coordinating monthly meetings on subjects that helped them better aid our clients. This job was by far my most challenging and rewarding. I say that because I truly loved what I did. I threw myself into it like there was no tomorrow. My criminal justice background helped tremendously with the police officers who saw me as one of them and not just an "outsider" trying to get my foot in the door. Of course the doughnuts I brought in by the dozens didn't hurt either! In fact, that kind of became a joke among the officers. I tried to always show up at briefing time and I always brought donuts along. After all, what police officer can resist coffee and donuts? Then while I had their attention, I would go over the previous night's events, new ideas, up-coming training, and so on. Before long, I had gained their respect, and soon they were willing to work with me and not against me.

Then during July of 2000, some truly ugly things began to occur at our office. First, between July 3 and July 5, 2000, someone entered our office building by key access and placed a letter addressed to one of our legal advocates on her desk in the legal office. This letter consisted of letters cut out of a magazine and pasted together which read, "Patricia no queers allowed here - get the hell out". This office along with all the legal filing cabinets were always locked at night by me before leaving due to the confidentiality of the files that were contained within. When Patricia found the letter, she notified our executive director. That director ordered a mandatory staff meeting for that Thursday at 1 p.m. Since I was sick that day and not at work, I was notified via phone that there was a mandatory meeting scheduled, and it was very important that everyone be there. I stressed that I was sick and would not be in, but was told everyone had to be there as it was a very important mandatory meeting. I decided to show up at the meeting and was advised about the incident and the letter. A photocopy of the letter was passed around for everyone to see. The director formally apologized on behalf of herself and the entire staff to Patricia stating that this kind of behavior would not be tolerated. She also advised everyone that she had contacted the prosecutor's office and the state police, a full investigation was going to be done and that whoever did this would be prosecuted to the fullest extent. She also stated that she would appreciate it if everyone would cooperate with the police in any way they were asked. I advised my supervisor that I would be returning home as I was still sick. At that point, our secretary walked out into the office to tell everyone that the state police would be in tomorrow to begin interviewing and fingerprinting people. I advised her that since it was my day off, I could be reached at home if they needed to speak to me. It was my understanding that on July 7, 2000 Sgt. Dixon and Sgt. Abbott of the State Police interviewed Patricia and numerous other staff members. It is also my understanding that there was a second incident which occurred between 5 p.m. on July 14th and 8 a.m. on July 17th. The supervisor walked into the legal office at approximately 8 a.m. and notice the Patricia's desk had been "trashed". The trash from her trash can had been dumped onto her desk, personal photographs, posters and other items that were hanging on the walls surrounding her desk had been ripped down and torn up along with personal items on her desk that were destroyed. In addition to that, her phone cord had been cut. The state police were again called out to investigate. They collected evidence, dusted for prints and again conducted interviews. At approximately 3:20 p.m. that afternoon, a supervisor came down to my office in the basement and asked if I had heard what happened. Since I had only just arrived and had not had an opportunity to talk to anyone yet, I said "No!" She sat down and began to tell me about the second incident.

On Monday, July 17th, Sgt. Dixon contacted me via pager to ask if I could come down to the post. I advised him that my truck was at the dealership being worked on and that I would not be able to go until the following day. He then asked me to stop by the post the next day.

The following day I drove to the post to see Sgt. Dixon. We met in his office. He asked if I knew why I was there and I stated, "I assume that you want to interview me." "No", he replied, I was not a suspect and in fact, he wanted my help. Because of my background, I had worked these kinds of cases before and he wanted to get my opinion on the situation. He also stated that he had asked me to come by the post because he did not want anyone back at the office to know we had spoken. He wanted to use me as a source if anyone said or did anything that might help them in solving this case. I agreed to do whatever I could, including providing a list of all the employees who had worked there and left since I started. He brought up the idea of a surveillance, which I also helped with if he was short of manpower. He then asked me if I had any idea who might have done something like this. "No", I answered, "I can't believe that anyone I work with could feel this way let alone do anything like this". Everyone had reacted with shock and disbelief when they heard about it, yet there was one person, Deedee who was very upset with the way the entire investigation was being handled. I told him that I felt Patricia and her partner should be eliminated first as it had always been my experience that it usually was the victim or someone close to her in these kind of situations. Oddly enough, Patricia had recently broken up with her partner and had just the day before announced that she would be leaving in mid-August to go to New York State to accept a volunteer position. He never asked me my whereabouts or questioned me about the dates involved. Later that day I called Sgt. Dixon back with a theory that he might consider. The first incident could have been some sort of practical joke. The second incident however, involved cutting, ripping, tearing, shredding, etc. These types of behaviors are signs of anger. My theory was that the second incident was done not to hurt Patricia, but in retaliation for Denise (Who was the Director of the Program) for bringing in the police and the prosecutor. He said, "That was something he had already considered which is why Deedee (another employee) was suspected; as she reacted with anger instead of shock. However, I told him, "That I did not believe that Deedee could have or would have done such a thing. Yes, she was angry, but over the way the entire investigation had been handled, and the fact that Denise left us the next day with no support or guidance from staff or board members. (She in fact, was out of town during both incidents)

On August 18, 2000 I was again contacted by a phone by Sgt. Dixon who advised me that my name had come up several times during the investigation due to the hours I worked. He stated that he had exhausted all other leads and the only thing left was to set up polygraph tests. I told him that I thought this was a good idea as it might bring forth the guilty party with just the threat of taking that step. He advised me that he had this test scheduled for the following Wednesday, which was August 23, and wanted to know if I would volunteer to take the first one.

His reasoning for this was with my background, and if I went first, the others would see that there was nothing to it, and follow along. In other words it would be encouraging them and making them more comfortable with the idea. I then advised him that I could not take the test due to my psychological history. I also told him I was on medication that would affect the results of the test. (I would not pass or fail the test, but the results would be inconclusive due to the medication). I told him if he thought it would help, he could tell her I had taken the test and pasted or if she asked me, I would tell her I taken it and passed. He seemed to appreciate that and stated, "I'm not aware of how they affect the test and that I will consult with the polygraph examiner and get back with you." He then told me, "If you don't hear back from me by Monday, give me a call."

During the next few days, I contacted several of Michigan's top polygraph experts. After explaining the situation to them, they all concurred with the following information. First, that Michigan had a Polygraph Protection Act which stated that I was "an at will employee", and, my employer could not make me take a test or fire me for refusing to take it. I could sue however, for wrongful termination or public policy violation. I was advised against taking the test because of the medications I was on as they would interfere with the outcome, thus making it less accurate. Furthermore, the results would not be admissible in any court of law. In addition, they gave me the names of several attorneys that they thought might be able to help me out. I contacted one of them and he stated that he would be more than happy to represent me if it came to that.

On the same day, I contacted the director of CRIS Information Services-Investigative Division, one of Michigan's top polygraph experts. I explained the situation to him, advising him of the medications I was taking and the dosages involved. He advised me against taking the test because of the medications stating that they would interfere with the results of the test making it inaccurate. Besides that, the results would not be admissible in court. He strongly advised me to get an attorney and recommended three by name.

Three days later, I contacted one of the attorneys at his home, and he advised me against taking the test for several reasons. First, the medications would affect the results and make the test inconclusive. Secondly, there is a state statute which allows employees to refuse to take such a test without fear of repercussions or being fired.

On the same day, I also contacted a second attorney by phone who advised me of the "Michigan Polygraph Protection Act". He stated that I am considered "an at will employee", and, my employer cannot make me take a test or fire me for refusing to take it. I could sue for wrongful termination or public policy violation. I should note at this point that both these attorneys said they would be willing to represent me and any other employee who would like representation.

On the next day, within five minutes of my arrival to work, Denise approached me and blatantly said, "I want to talk to you in my office now". After entering the office she asked, Jane, the secretary to leave the room. After Jane left, Denise closed the door and placed bricks against the bottom of the door. I jokingly asked if I should be concerned that she was barricading me into her office. "No", she stated, "I am having trouble keeping the door shut so I use the bricks to keep the door closed for privacy" We sat down at the table and she advised me that the investigation was continuing and that this whole thing was taking far too long, so the next step would be polygraph tests. She went on further to state that test had been set up for tomorrow, which was Wednesday, August 23, and that she wanted me to take one. I asked her if she had talked to Sgt. Dixon recently and after hesitating, she said, "No". I advised her that she should talk to him because we had spoken on Friday and again on Monday. I would not take the test. She inquired as to why, and I again explained that I was not a suspect and that due to my depression, I was on medications that would make the test inconclusive. I also advised her that I had spoken to polygraph experts, my physician, and two attorneys, all of whom had advised me against taking the test. She then requested the name and phone number of my physician and said she wanted to speak to her personally. I willingly provided her with that information, but told her that my doctor would not discuss my case with her without a signed medical release form. She then wanted me to sign a medical release form allowing my doctor to discuss my condition with her. I gave her the name and number of my physician, but refused to sign a consent form. I also immediately sent a letter to my doctor in writing and by fax requesting that she not give out any information without my written consent. She then leaned forward and stated, "You realize if you don't take this test, that that it will affect your job here?" "No", I said, "it will affect your job and the continued existence of this organization." I then stood up and said," You'll have to excuse me, this conversation is now over."

From that point on it seemed like it was them against me. Denise did everything she could to make my life miserable. I was beginning to wonder if this was what I really wanted to do. Was it worth trying to prove my innocence at the rate of being so miserable and unhappy? At least I had other things that I could think about that made me happy, like planning a wedding and carrying on a long distance relationship with Wayne. It was time to concentrate more on those things than the problems that were going on around me at work.

However the problems continued to mount during the months that followed and working in that kind of environment, was very tense and stressful. The following week I had a meeting scheduled with Denise and Emily to discuss grants and the use of money throughout the coming year for the on-call and legal programs.

Instead of discussing that though, I was informed that I would be changing positions and locations. I was moved to another location, my keys where taken away from me, access to files where restricted, 75% of my job responsibilities were taken away from me, and so on.

Denise wasn't interested in hearing my explanations, instead she told me "Pack and move my stuff, end of meeting." On the 19th I moved my belongings to the other office and was informed that the locks on the administration building had all been changed. I asked Emily, my supervisor, why we were now just changing the locks when so many of us had suggested it back in July when the first incident had originally taken place. She had no answer other than Denise, our director, had the locks changed today. I then turned in my set of keys. On October 26 we had our regular monthly staff meeting at 12:30 PM in the administration building. Denise was not there because her dad had had a stroke that morning. Near the end of the meeting, Brittany, our special shift supervisor, advised everyone that she had something she wanted to say. She was extremely upset with the way people were treating me, talking about me behind my back, backstabbing me, starting rumors, etc. She stated that she didn't care what they had thought about me or what I may or may not have done, but that it was detrimental to me and the others by causing such problems. She went on to say how upset I had been the Saturday before, how this had brought me to the point of tears and even threatening to quit effective immediately. She expressed how important my program was in that we could not afford to lose me in addition to the dozens of others that would have left. She told them that they owed me an apology and that we were all supposed to be there for each other not attacking or singling out one person based on rumors or suspicions. While I was not aware that she was going to do that, I truly was grateful that someone had the guts to stand up and finally say something. I personally thanked her after the meeting for being so brave and make such a statement.

I informed Denise that we had room for possibly three more desks in addition to my own. She stated, "No I feel that crisis call takers are the first responders to people who call our crisis lines and you are a first responder to the scenes therefore we should be located in the same building." Move your stuff. End of meeting.

I along with the others, firmly believed I was forced to move from the administration building to the shelter because a lesbian had been recently hired and she would be working in the basement where my old office was. It appeared that they still considered me a suspect, and thought by making my job more difficult and harassing me, that I might quit. It didn't work however. I continued to work on and do my job to the best of my abilities given the circumstances.

Late on January 4th, I showed up at the office just as I would on every other night. Upon arriving at there, I noticed that I had a message on my desk from Gordon, a good friend and police officer with whom I had worked with. He was a sergeant with one of the local police departments who had done a lot to help get our program up and running. When I called him back it was obvious that he was going through some sort of crisis. After talking with him for some time, it became apparent that he had been drinking. I was concerned because he sounded suicidal over an incident with the mother of his children. I told him that I had some good news and needed to meet with him in person. I left the office planning on being back by 11 PM and telling the staff that if something came up and I couldn't get back by than that I would call. When I got to Gordon's house, my suspicions that he had been drinking were confirmed. We talked for about an hour before his crises was defused. He then got around to asking me about my good news.

"Hey" he said, "What were you going to tell me?"

"I'm getting married," I said cheerfully, "And I'd like to ask you if you would do me the honor of giving me away?"

His eyes got teary, a wide smile came over his face and he held out his arms to give me a hug me as he said, "The honor is all mine my friend. This calls for a drink."

"Oh no", I said, "I can't, I'm working".

"Come on just one before you leave," he said, as he poured a drink.

"I think you're trying to get me fired," I said as I took a couple of sips of the drink and looked for a place to put it down.

"No, but this is the best news I've heard all day. Thanks for taking time to come over, listen to my problems and include me in the most important day of your life. You really are a good friend."

"Yeah, yeah ...where have I heard that before?" I said as I headed for the door. "Have a good night. I'll have Wayne call you after my surgery." I said. (I was scheduled to have Tubal Ligation Surgery.)

Except I didn't just have my tubes "tied" so to speak. I actually had the doctor cut out sections of the tubes on each side and then tie them. I wanted to make sure there was absolutely no way on this earth that I could ever get pregnant. Every doctor I had consulted with had refused the procedure, saying I was too young and that I might change my mind. I was now 35 years young and engaged to be married to a man with five children, who was 23 years older than me. Since neither of us wanted more children, my doctor finally agreed to do the procedure.

There were only a few cars on the road as I headed home, the snow was falling lightly with an occasional gust of wind. As I was exiting I-96 onto US 23 a car came out of nowhere and cut me off. I swerved to avoid hitting him. I slid on some ice, striking a marker pole, before landing in the ditch. Unable to get out on my own, I called for assistance and asked for a tow truck. Shortly thereafter two Michigan State Troopers arrived to help. Recognizing me, one of them asked me to step out of my SUV. At first I didn't want to as it was very cold out and I was wearing a dress with high heels. My vehicle was in a snowbank and I didn't want to leave a heated vehicle until the tow truck came. He asked again saying you're welcome to sit in my car if you like. Not thinking anything of it, I opened the door and went to step out of the truck. The snow was deeper than I expected so I had grabbed the door to prevent myself from falling.

"Have you been drinking?" He said.

Not wanting to lie and knowing that I had only had a small amount, I said, "Why yes, but only one. Then realizing how that must have sounded I said, "Guess that's what they all say, huh?"

"Then you won't mind taking a breathalyzer right?" He said?

Now, I starting to get upset. I was tired, cold and hungry. I hadn't eaten all day. I was also on call for the night. Were these two serious or just trying to give me such a hard time?

(In spite of developing excellent relations with most of the police departments and personnel, there were still a few officers, as luck would have it, that did not like me and the work I was doing.)

"Here you go you know how to do this. Blow" he said as he held the breathalyzer in front of my mouth.

"Well, looks like you're spending the night in jail." He said.

"Oh come on. Be *serious*!" I said with a touch of anger in my voice. I told you I only had one drink and I just came from the Sarges house. You can call him to verify it."

"You'll get your phone call. Right now you're under arrest. So put your hands behind your back." He turned me around and put the handcuffs on so tight that they actually hurt. He then sat me in the car. (The next day I developed black and blue marks on my wrists where the cuffs had been).

I was taken back to the station where I was fingerprinted and placed in a cell till morning. As I sat in the cell, I realized that what I had done, was a mistake. I did not think that one drink, one sip or two, would lead to all this. The next morning I was given another breathalyzer, allowed to make a phone call (which I made to Wayne my fiancée) and taken to court for my arraignment. When we walked out of the court room Wayne gave me a hug and all I could do was cry, but in the safety and love of his arms I knew everything would be ok. He truly was my Shinning Knight in Armor (a kick name I had given him when we first met). Thank goodness he had been staying at my house as I was about to have my surgery and he had agreed to take care of me while I recovered.

Thank God he was there for me, because this was just the beginning of a series of bad and unfortunate things that were to happen to me.

Chapter 14

What Now?

I was now a "criminal with a record". Little did I know that this one event was going to turn out to be the best thing that could have happened to me? I ended up losing my job about two weeks later. I put my home in Michigan up for sale and it sold in fairly quickly. I think I closed on it around the 1st of March and then moved to Maryland to live with Wayne. We began to plan our wedding which was set for June 9, 2001. It was to be held at Faith Lutheran Church in Grand Blanc, Michigan. We traveled back and forth to meet with the Pastor, the wedding coordinator, the director of music, and my best friend, Ursula, who was to be my maid of honor. Traveling back and forth was fun and allowed us to make all the necessary arrangements. I was so excited and busy with the details of the wedding. While this was my second marriage, I considered it my first. (The first one was annulled through both the church and state.) I did not have the opportunity to have a "true in-church wedding" the first time around. It was so refreshing and wonderful to make plans with my best friend and my mother, both of whom were not part of my "first marriage".

It wasn't long after I made that move to Maryland that I

knew, "something was wrong". I began to see both mental and physical changes. I began to think to myself, "What have I done?" Is this a mistake?" First of all, it was hard for me to live on a farm. I felt like I was so isolated and far away from everything. Next, we were living in a basement apartment that was very dark. Even with the lights on, it felt gloomy to me. I was so use to brightly lit rooms. Then there was, and this is going to sound strange at first, the sleeping arrangements. Before we had a chance to set up my bed, we used Wayne's twin bed to sleep in. I didn't realize it at first, but subconsciously I think I was uncomfortable as I was thinking back to when I was a child in my grandfather's bed. I would find myself crying or cleaning for hours. (These were things I would later recognize as tell-tale signs of mania for me) I also began to put on weight as I would eat whenever I got stressed.

I finally snapped one night threatening to shoot myself. I had decided to leave, but Wayne tried to stop me by standing in front of my vehicle. I thought if I held the gun to my head I could frighten him into moving so that I could leave. It didn't work though. I ended up leaving on foot. As I rushed down the street, I ran and pounded on someone's front door to ask them to call the police for me. They did, however after a short conversation with the police, they convinced me to return home. It was there that I had another conversation with them and ended up going to the ER for a psych evaluation. All that was going through my mind was, "Oh No, Not another one! What's the use?" I did go and the ER doctor kept me there for a few hours then finally let me go home later that night with the stipulation that I follow-up with a psychiatrist the following week.

I had been to dozens of psychiatrists before, and none of them had ever helped. But I had promised I would go, so I did. The doctor listened patiently to my long history dating back as early as I could remember. Then came the long list of diagnoses. His face was stern as I rattled off them one by one; Dissociative Amnesia, Affective Disorder, Anxiety Disorder, Schizoaffective Disorder, Adjustment Disorder, Post-Traumatic Stress Disorder, Major Depressive Disorder, Dysthymia, Somatization Disorder, Psychological Factors, Affecting Physical Condition, Hypochondriasis, Antisocial Personality Disorder, Schizoid Personality Disorder, Disassociate Fugue and Borderline Personality Disorder.

I glanced up as I ended the long list and took a deep breath. Phew, try getting that all out in one breath!

The doctor folded his hands and shook his head. I really don't understand why no one caught this before, but it's very obvious to me, you're bipolar."

I laughed out loud and said, "Well that's a first! I think I've been labeled just about everything but that! How can you be so sure?"

"As I said" he said, "It's obvious. Now what we have to do is get you started on the right medications and see you they are stabilized and monitored. And the only way to do that is to have you hospitalized. You'll have to go to John Hopkins right away." My husband and I looked at each other. Oh no, I thought! I don't want to go to the hospital. Give me whatever medications you want, but I'm not going to any hospital. That will definitely push me over the edge! I don't want to lose my job, leave my cats or my house. I need that security.

Wayne chimed in at that point and said, "Please, I'll help her with whatever monitoring of the medications that she needs. She just got this job. She's working as a Custodian at a school. It really means a lot to her. You know what'll happen if they find out that she's bipolar. Oh, and she has cats that are her kids. Please, if you take away all she has, she won't do well at all. Can't she stay home?"

"It's not just the medications", the doctor said, "but her moods will have to be closely monitored as well. You will have to keep a log and stay in touch with me. Agree?"

"Yes," We both said as we looked at each other nodding.

"Okay then, let's start you on them tonight" the doctor said as he began to write out several prescriptions. "We're going to start slow and then increase them as long as you don't have any bad side effects."

Wayne and I left his office and headed toward our pharmacy. We traveled for several blocks in silence before I finally asked, "So what do you think of him?"

"I think he really wants to help you," he replied. "I've had twenty some years of doctors who really wanted to help me", I said. "I sure hope this guy proves to be different."

It was then that I was first diagnosed as being bipolar. For those of you who are not familiar with Bipolar Disorder, it is brain and behavior disorder characterized by severe shifts in a person's mood and energy that make it difficult for a person to function. These cyclic episodes are punctuated by normal moods.

I personally can't help but wonder why no one saw the signs or symptoms in me any sooner, for I clearly demonstrated almost ALL of them. And while I will list the symptoms shortly, I want to first say how difficult it was to write this chapter.

It still amazes me that it took so long. I had been suffering from depression and anxiety since I was a teenager. There had been suicide attempts, cognitive, emotional, physical, somatic and interpersonal issues throughout my entire life. I had been to see what seemed like dozens upon dozens of doctors and psychiatrists throughout the years. Each gave me a different diagnosis and different

155

medications to try. Nothing had worked. Nothing that was until that doctor in Maryland. I have been told over and over again that you must find the "right doctor and have the right medications" if you are going to manage your illness. Without that combination you are just spinning your wheels and getting discouraged. How true that is.

I must say, though, that being bipolar has had its toll on me in many ways. For example, as a young woman sexuality was like a drug for me. By the time I was 35 when I was first diagnosed as being bipolar, I had lost track of the number of people with whom I had slept. I would swing back and forth between being depressed and needing sex. The riskier it was, the better. I didn't know until my diagnosis that having multiple sex partners, thinking about sex constantly, having one night stands or being so interested in pornography were symptoms, and that, if I had the proper treatment, those symptoms would disappear. My life of hypersexuality was particularly dangerous, for which I am now deeply sorry. I had affairs with married men, participated in threesomes, had same-sex encounters and even sex in public.

I went on shopping sprees, running up my credit cards by buying things I didn't need, all the while without considering my financial situation. These purchases were based on emotional feelings rather than rational ones. I am in no way excusing my actions, but I know now what

I did was a symptom of my condition that could have, and did, hurt others.

Shortly after I began taking my new medications, I started feeling better. The transformation was amazing. I would say it was a little over a week when I noticed a difference. The doctor had to do some adjusting, but they helped tremendously. <u>I mean really, like night and day!</u>

Shortly after that, I found out that my mother's health was declining. She was living alone in Florida, so we made the decision to move to Florida where we could be closer to her. It turned out to be the best thing for all of us.

The move meant looking for a house. We found an agent we liked and began searching online. It wasn't long before we found our dream home. We picked that house for several reasons. One, because it was large enough for my mom and us when she needed our twenty-four hour care. It happened sooner than we expected. It was only a short time after we moved in, that my mother was diagnosed with lung cancer. She had started coughing, so I took her to the doctor thinking she had bronchitis or pneumonia. Once there, the doctor decided to send her for an x-ray. Our world drastically changed the day she called us to say they had spotted cancer in one of her lungs. The doctor wanted us to go and see an Oncologist as soon as possible. Mom was hesitant at first saying, "I don't want to go through chemo and radiation." After meeting with the Doctor she decided to give it a try for "me". I surely would be there for her throughout it all. I took her to each treatment, and after we would go to lunch or just stop to have coffee and watch the people. Mom didn't have much. When I first came down to Florida she was living in a small apartment and was on welfare. As much as she hated the chemotherapy, she looked forward to our lunches together.

Our dream home was not far from where my mother lived. It had a beautiful yard with lots of trees and flowers which none of the other houses had. It was already handicapped accessible with an extra bedroom and bathroom for Mom. She stayed in her apartment as long as she could, but when it became obvious that she could no longer care for herself, we had to make a decision. Either we had to take her in or put her in a nursing home. I was not about to put her in a nursing home.

She had a cat at the time that was as big and mean as they come. His name was, Pussy Cat. One day Mom and I had to have "the talk". I never thought that day would come, but there we were in my living room. She was not doing well on her own and her doctor said it was time. I wanted to give Mom the choice, so I began to explain to her that we had moved here with the intention of taking care of her and emphasized that she could move in with us, have her own room, bathroom, continue to keep her car and cat, or she could go to the nursing home where she would only be allowed to take some clothes and a few personal items. Needless to say, she moved in with us. It was nice having her here because I didn't have to worry about her. I was able to get a good job within weeks of moving to this beautiful, sunny state. And since my husband was retired and I worked second shift, we had the perfect set up with which to care for her. We could literally have someone with her 24 hours a day and yet allow her to have her "space and freedoms about the house". Something she couldn't have in a nursing home.

Mom lived with us for several months. During this time, Mom and I became much closer. We had been estranged for so many years that we had much to mend. Wayne and I finally found that she could be a most enjoyable person. In October 2004, she started going downhill. She remained strong willed but cheerful up to the end.

Then one day she began to have difficulties breathing, so we called the Hospice nurse in to check on her. She came to the house, and did an exam. She then gave her some extra morphine to control her fidgeting and help her sleep. She came out again later that night and gave her more morphine. Once she finally drifted off to sleep, I gently kissed her on the forehead and then went to my bedroom to sleep. I slept fitfully during the night.

I was tuckered out from the night before so Wayne, letting me sleep, was the first one up to check on her. He went into her room and found she had died peacefully during the night.

Now that mom had died, Wayne and I had to make some other important life change decisions. We had come down mainly to take care of Mom and have given little thought to the future. A large emotional weight had just been removed from our shoulders. What were we to do? We now determined we could stay in Florida with no obligations…

Then we realized that something amazing had happened!

After we moved to Florida, my moods improved! I mean, really improved! One thing I could attribute it to, was the sunshine and a bigger, brighter house. Could it be that simple? I had heard that light could affect mood, but had never considered it with regards to mine. Now I seemed to have evidence that it was true. One could actually see the difference in photographs of me. I looked happier and healthier in the Florida photos. But I think it was more than that. I believe I was happy because I was happily married and now had healed my relationship with my deceased Mother, a job I liked and for the first time in my life, felt normal.

Was that possible?

Chapter 15

Grandpa

Grandpa Phillip Stiles

I decided to put this chapter at the end because this person, my good Grandpa, like me, also had secrets. They not only shaped his life, but made him a better person. He was not only my hero, but my Grandpa. Grandpa Stiles, was my mother's father. He was a kind, gentle, hardworking man.

As a child I was mesmerized by his large ears and his innate ability to wiggle them while he talked or did anything for that matter. To this day, I have not figured how he did it. But it sure brought hours of laughter and joy to our time together. I also remember him teaching me how to fish. He and Grandma lived on a lake in Fenton, Michigan. Grandpa and I would often sit on the end of the dock for what seemed like hours holding our poles waiting to catch the infamous "big one". These are special memories that I will forever treasure.

But like me, Grandpa's secret began during his childhood. He was born in Birmingham, England on May 12, 1899. He started school like every other child about the age of 5. However, within a short period of time, both of his parents died. That left Phillip's older brother, Harry, and his sister, May, as his guardians. Together they then made a decision that would forever change Phillip's life. Phillip would take part in the British child scheme. He ultimately became one of the approximately 118,000 children that would be sent to Canada under the little-known Child Immigration Scheme from 1863-1939. These children came from England, Scotland, Ireland, The Isle of Man and Wales,

Together they felt that Phillip would be better off if they sent him to Canada where he would have a fresh new life complete with parents to care for him. The two of them decided that young Phillip should go to Canada where they thought he would have a better life. So on May 24, 1910, Phillip, who was 1 of 153 children, boarded a ship along with no one else he knew. The good ship Mongolian left Liverpool and set sail for Halifax, Nova Scotia. He was headed for the John T. Middlemore Home in Halifax, Nova Scotia, Canada where he thought he was going to be adopted.

Instead, the children would be sent to Canadian farms under contract. The terms would require that children be housed, fed, clothed, and sent to school. A small fee would be paid for fostering younger children, older children would help with chores, and more extended labor would be required from adolescents. At 18, the terms of indenture were to be discharged. Canada was marketed, to the parents and the children, as a haven within the storms of their lives where money grew on trees and the adventure of travelling to a land where cowboys and lumberjacks were, sounded appealing. The parents were relieved that a way had been found where their children would be safe and healthy.

However, the harsh truth was that the monitoring of children's placements was often neglected, and many children found themselves essentially abandoned to new lives which were worse than the old. Siblings were separated. Girls assisted farm wives not only with housework and children, but on the fields, as well. Boys became farm workers who were grossly overworked.

While some of the children were indeed accepted into the families they worked for and were practically adopted, many of these children suffered. Children could be 'returned' and reassigned. Many were moved from one farm to another. Some ran away or simply disappeared; some died from ill-health or injuries resulting from neglect and abuse, and some committed suicide. [R8]

We know this was the case with Grandpa, for at the age of fifteen he tried to run away to join the army. They would not allow him to join, so he went back to work on the farm. When he turned sixteen, he ran away and tried to enlist again. However, once again he was turned away. Finally in November of 1915, he enlisted in the Canadian Over Seas Expeditionary Force and served until July of 1919. He spent time at Wimereux, France convalescing from a gunshot wound to the upper right arm. He was discharged in July of 1919. From there he was able to locate his brother-in-law in Glasgow, Scotland where he worked in a tire retreading business. He then returned to Canada in 1922, but eventually traveled to the United States in May of 1923. Records show he settled in Fenton, Michigan and began working for a large gas company. Soon after that, he meet his first wife, Katherine Friedmann. They married November 25, 1926. They would be the proud parents of five daughters; Suzanne, Judy, Francis, Margaret (my mother) and Hanna. Which brings us back to the original five girls we started my memoir with. Now we know why he spoke so very little of his childhood. He taught us all the meaning of hard work and dreaming big.

Now that many of the family's secrets and lies have been exposed, let's consider some of the lessons learned from them.

Chapter 16

Life Lessons

"The only person you are destined to become is the person you decide to be."

I asked at the end of Chapter 14 whether is it possible to change your life and feel normal?

Ok, so now you may be saying, "She's just told us all her deepest, darkest secrets and lies. Aside from it being good reading, why on earth would a person do that?" Well, because hopefully I have your attention, and perhaps I have you pondering your own family's secrets and lies, the question arises, how can you make a difference? The answer, surprising enough, is simple. I do not mean that it will be easy, I do mean that it can be done. Below are several steps that can help begin the healing process.

I feel that our society has been going in the wrong direction for years. First, prayer is no longer allowed in schools. And don't get me wrong, I'm not saying you have to pray to God here, but at least have a moment of silence where you acknowledge (or not) whomever or whatever it is that you believe in.

Second, the pledge of allegiance has been removed from our schools. We live in a great country, a country that has given us Life, Liberty, and the pursuit of Happiness. We should acknowledge this truth by the pledge of allegiance whenever possible, starting in school. Whether you were born here, or immigrated, your allegiance is to America first. Be proud of your heritage, BUT pledge your allegiance to America.

Third, corporal punishment, while still on the books, is not used in most schools for fear of children or parents suing. Instead of allowing some reasonable corporal punishment, schools are left with discipline policies which create a less reliable climate for the students and staff.

Another example, would be denying some access to electronics. Have you walked into a restaurant lately and looked around? Take a look at the table next to you with the family of say four, all of which are sitting with faces buried in their phones or computers. There is no conversation going on, no interaction, just the beginning of carpal tunnel syndrome. It's sad.

Here's another example. Have you ever gone to your favorite restaurant when the computer has crashed? Try to have that teenager give you the right change or the right food order for that matter. Makes you wonder what happened to learning the basics in life: Reading, 'Riting and 'Rithmetic. Many of the young children at the elementary school where I work, don't even know how to tie their own shoes. I don't know about you, but when I was growing up that was one of the first things I had to learn.

Then there is the issue of broken families. Families can break up and split up for a variety of reasons. This leads to the children being raised by single parents, grandparents, stepparents or others who might not even be related to them. These children are more likely to develop emotional issues, harbor resentment, experience loneliness, depression or have difficulties in school. If we, as a society, can recognize these issues _when_ they arise early on, then we have a chance of preventing a lifetime of pain and suffering for millions of people. I, for example, can still remember the day my parents spit up and my siblings just "disappeared". They were simply there one day and gone the next. There was no warning, no explanation, nothing! How on earth does a six year old deal with that? Well, because children have little cognitive ability at that point, they often blame themselves. They may also feel it is their responsibility to bring their parents back together.

As I grew older into my teens and saw that wasn't going to happen, I went on to blame my mother for everything. It was her fault that my siblings were gone. It was her fault that my parents divorced. It was her fault that Dad lost his job. It was her fault that Dad was an alcoholic. It was her fault that I had to live with my grandparents. It was her fault that I was depressed. EVERYTHING was her fault as far as I was concerned! Needless to say, this lead to a very strained, impossible relationship between us. We literally went almost 10 years without talking to one another.

Finally, I came to a point in my life where I said, "I can't allow this bitterness and anger to keep eating me up like this", for it was doing exactly that. I realized if I was to ever move forward, I must first move backward and deal with the past. And that for me, meant forgiving her. Something I wasn't particularly good at, because it was so much easier to blame her then forgive. Usually everyone somewhere along the way blames another for something. (Please understand that forgiving doesn't necessarily mean that you approve or excuse everything that person did) I soon realized that I had to make those I wanted to forgive "human" so that I could better understand why they were the way they were. I started with my mother. After many years of not talking, I finally was able to forgive her and I **slowly** rebuilt our mother/daughter relationship.

That was about the time I began to plan my wedding. It was important for me to have her in my life. Needless to say, we both worked hard at it and in the end, she was there to see her daughter walk down the aisle. Then a few years later she was diagnosed with stage four lung cancer. At first she said she didn't want to go through any type of treatment. Then when we met with the oncologist and he explained that she would be able to live longer with the treatments. She looked at me with tears in her eyes and said, "Then I'll do it. I owe my daughter, who I wasn't there for when she needed me, but I can be here for her now." Every emotion I could imagine welled up in me at that point and I couldn't help but cry with her. She had given me the best gift ever . . . Time, precious time, so very precious time to live together as mother and daughter. As you know, when she was finally no longer able to care for herself, she moved in with us and lived there until she passed away. I am so glad that I was able to forgive her when I did and rebuild our relationship. Thanks Mom!

So what have I learned? For one thing, that life is precious and short. There isn't time to be angry or resentful. If you have been victimized in any way, shape or form, please get help! Don't waste time holding grudges or being angry.

I truly believe another thing we as a nation have to do, is see that everyone has health care. And I do mean EVERYONE! Mental Illness is just one aspect of health care that needs attention. The mentally ill have nowhere to go. The lucky ones have family. The others end up in emergency rooms, county jails or the streets. The unlucky ones end up in the morgue. States have been closing mental hospitals for decades. I spent, like many others, years searching for the right diagnosis and the right medication. Health care shouldn't make that harder, but easier. People need to feel free to openly seek treatment without fear of any repercussions, be it stigma, loss of job, and so on. Since we know that mental illness often runs genetically, we should begin to look for it at a young age. The younger we can detect it, the better it will be for the person and those surrounding them. When it comes to mental illnesses, I believe we have to overhaul our entire health care system. If everyone had health insurance and there was no longer any stigma associated with mental illness, we would have less problems. If a person is diagnosed with a mental illness there should be a team approach that would allow care from a number of different sources.

For example, let's take me. Say I am diagnosed as being bi-polar. I should have a primary care doctor, a psychiatrist and a family member or friend who wishes to be my advocate. This advocate would be responsible for monitoring me. That would include my daily moods, medications, transportation to doctor appointments, and any other medical or legal necessities. That "responsible party" would then report any problems that they encounter with me. If that person notices something unusual in my behavior, or suspects that I am not taking my medications, than they should be able to consult with my doctors and or the police without any fear of repercussions. People have to begin to care about one another again and not be afraid to "get involved". This "team approach" would not only cut down on crime, but help those who go undiagnosed. With such laws enacted, spouses, family members and friends would be more willing to take responsibility for their loved ones once they are diagnosed with a mental illness.

Likewise, pharmaceutical companies need to work much better at keeping the cost of medication down, so that all people have access to the right medications. It shouldn't just be available to those who have insurance. Because what happens to those who are homeless? Or have no insurance?

The same goes for our Veterans. Many come back with mental and or physical challenges. Many find it difficult to transition from the military back to civilian life. Think about it. Is this how we really want to treat our military personnel and those that keep us safe from harm's way? They who help give us our priceless freedom? They deserve a home, health care and help transitioning back into civilian life.

As I think back over my life, I realize now that I went into law enforcement because I wanted to help people. But throughout my career, I continued to see bad things happening to good people. Why was this? I choose to think they are meant to be eye openers.

I believe that people don't change unless they want to or they have to, and we can't do it for them. I continued to have negative events in my life, but wasn't paying attention to them like I should have been. They were merely "bumps in the road" so to speak, yet it was my bipolar diagnosis that really knocked me for a loop. It caused me the loss of my job and eventually ended my fifteen year career. All my life I had dreamed of having a "family" that didn't involve me actually having a child.

When I met my husband that dream came true. I am now blessed with an incredible, loving and supportive family. I never wanted children of my own because I feared my children would end up with a mental illness or cancer since both ran so strongly in my family. I therefore made a conscious choice to not put a person through a life of either of those medical or psychological hells. Better to break the cycle I thought, by not having any children. To this day, I am sure I made the right choice.

I can honestly say I am no longer the same person I was 20 years ago. I recognize that I made mistakes and acted inappropriately. I had a disease that I let go uncontrolled and unmedicated. Thus, it controlled me and everything I did. People *can* start over if they have the right support systems to help them. I have been very fortunate to have my faith, family and friends. (The three F's)

This is only one piece of the pie. Our schools, law enforcement, government, religious leaders, and physicians need to work together as a team to advocate on behalf of those who are victims of mental health, sexual assault or domestic violence. We can't continue to have shootings at schools, malls, universities, and various other places. Please help me by empowering and educating your friends, family and governmental officials.

Take that first step. You too, can make a difference.

If You Try!

"The only person you are destined to become is the person you decide to be."

Yes, YOU!

Love and Blessings,

Bella

Epilogue

Hurricane Irma

I've often wondered if people were going to remember me, using just one word, what would it be. I would like to think they would say, she was a "Survivor".

For days my husband and I prepared for Hurricane Irma. We'd been through several hurricanes in our 17 years of life here in Florida so we felt as prepared as one could be. We had plenty of gas, water, food and other supplies. Our house had hurricane shutters, a generator, etc. As Sunday, September 10, 2017 neared, both family and friends called and texted us to ask, "Have you evacuated yet? Are you in a shelter? Are you safe? When we explained that we were choosing to stay, we had many people on pins and needles and worried sick about us. Both my husband and I tried to comfort them as the impending storm loomed closer. But this storm was different.

Hurricane Irma was an extremely powerful and catastrophic Cape Verde type hurricane, the most_intense observed in the Atlantic since Dean in 2007. It was also the most intense Atlantic hurricane to strike the

United States since Katrina in 2005, and the first major hurricane to make landfall in the state of Florida since Wilma in 2005. The ninth named storm, fourth hurricane, and second major hurricane of the 2017 Atlantic hurricane season, Irma caused widespread and catastrophic damage throughout its long lifetime, particularly in parts of the northeastern Caribbean and the Florida Keys. [R9]

Oddly though, one of the things I was most worried about at the time was my book. It was due to be sent to my publisher on the 11th. I had spent nearly 3 years working on it and after watching all the news coverage about Hurricane Irma, I was getting nervous. Irma had now changed her course and was heading right for us. What if we lost power? Were flooded? I had back-up copies I planned to take with me in the event we had to evacuate, but what if the unforeseen happened and I didn't make? "Better plan for that just in case", I thought. I decided in the event that something happened to me or the book, that I would send a copy to my sister. As the winds roared outside, my husband worked feverishly to email my sister a copy of my book. She lived outside Florida and I knew I could trust her to do it for me. "Please see that it gets published for me." I asked of her. With that weight off my shoulders I now felt ready to take on the storm. Luckily the storm again changed courses and spared us a direct hit. We had one large tree come down, lost many of our banana trees, had lots of debris from other trees strewn throughout the yard and our power was out for only a short period of time. We were among the VERY lucky ones!

Thank the Good Lord I didn't need to take my sister up on my request. But that does bring me back to why I think he gave me that strength to get through yet another difficult predicament. Throughout my life I have undergone many situations which have left me emotionally, physically and psychologically scared. Two things could have happened.

First, I could have crawled into a shell and been wounded for life. I could have tried to hide my past from everyone, but no amount of medications, drugs or alcohol would have made me feel "normal". I still would feel lonely and have trouble with relationships.

Or second, I could learn from my experiences, heal and move forward. I chose the second. By doing so successfully I make myself a "survivor". I have made my past a positive part of my identity. I hope by now writing about these experiences to inspire others that healing is possible and that you too can make a difference. If you try!

References

R1   Pg. 10 - Margaret Dempsey v. Gregory Dempsey
Bill of Complaint for Divorce - Genesee County
Courts, May 09, 1960

R2   Pg. 13 - Margaret Dempsey v Gregory Dempsey
Report on Petition to Amend Judgement of
Divorce - Genesee County Courts, Dec 28, 1966

R3   Pg. 16 - Handwritten Letter from Margaret
Zimmerman to her Dad and Caroline Stiles -
Dated July 08, 1965

R4   Pg. 26 - Neil Zimmerman v Connie Zimmerman -
Genesee County Courts

R5   Pg. 32 - Newspaper Article/Photo taken from
Flint Journal - Nov. 09, 1968

R6   Pg. 56 - Article titled Pediatric Sleepwalking from
Website: "Healthline" - Medically Reviewed by
Steven Kim on November 23, 2015 - Written by
Janelle Martel

R7   Pg. 109 - Roman Catholic Canon Laws – laws for
Annulment

R8   Pg. 163 - British Home Children, Article by
Lori   Oschefski – Advocacy & Research
Association

R9   Pg. 175 - Hurricane Irma – Wikipedia – The
Free Encyclopedia